Growing in the Gospel

THE PSALMS PROJECT VOLUME 1

Discovering the Spiritual World through the Psalms – Psalm 1 to 10

Michael Harvey Koplitz

TABLE OF CONTENTS

The Goal of this project:

This research project will examine the 150 psalms for the spiritual awareness each Psalm offers. Each Psalm will be examined by its language and the commentary of the Sages. The spiritual awareness analysis will be done in alignment with Ari's definition of the Tree of life, the Book of Creation, and the Zohar. Each verse of the Psalm will be rewritten using the intent of the language and spiritual commentary to convey its spiritual lesson.

The Main Resources:

The Zohar

The Book of Creation

Ari's writing on the Tree of Life and the Ten Sefirot

The Theological Wordbook of the Old Testament

Samson Hirsch's commentary on the Psalms

Tehillim – Psalms – A new translation with a commentary anthologized from the Talmudic and rabbinic sources

Accordance Bible Software

Language

New American Standard 1995	Hebrew
[1] How blessed is the man who does not walk in the counsel of the wicked, nor stand in the path of sinners, nob sit in the seat of scoffers! [2] But his delight is in the law of the LORD, and in His law he meditates day and night. [3] He will be like a tree *firmly* planted by [1]streams of water, which yields its fruit in its season and its leaf does not wither; and in whatever he does, he prospers. [4] The wicked are not so, but they are like chaff which the wind drives away. [5] Therefore the wicked will not stand in the judgment, nor sinners in the assembly of the righteous. [6] For the LORD knows the way of the righteous, but the way of the wicked will perish.	1 אַשְׁרֵי־הָאִישׁ אֲשֶׁר ׀ לֹא הָלַךְ בַּעֲצַת רְשָׁעִים וּבְדֶרֶךְ חַטָּאִים לֹא עָמָד וּבְמוֹשַׁב לֵצִים לֹא יָשָׁב: 2 כִּי אִם בְּתוֹרַת יְהֹוָה חֶפְצוֹ וּבְתוֹרָתוֹ יֶהְגֶּה יוֹמָם וָלָיְלָה: 3 וְהָיָה כְּעֵץ שָׁתוּל עַל־פַּלְגֵי מָיִם אֲשֶׁר פִּרְיוֹ ׀ יִתֵּן בְּעִתּוֹ וְעָלֵהוּ לֹא־יִבּוֹל וְכֹל אֲשֶׁר־יַעֲשֶׂה יַצְלִיחַ: 4 לֹא־כֵן הָרְשָׁעִים כִּי אִם־כַּמֹּץ אֲשֶׁר־תִּדְּפֶנּוּ רוּחַ: 5 עַל־כֵּן ׀ לֹא־יָקֻמוּ רְשָׁעִים בַּמִּשְׁפָּט וְחַטָּאִים בַּעֲדַת צַדִּיקִים: 6 כִּי־יוֹדֵעַ יְהֹוָה דֶּרֶךְ צַדִּיקִים וְדֶרֶךְ רְשָׁעִים תֹּאבֵד:

Psalm One Targum

Psa. 1:1 Happy the man who has not walked in the council of the wicked, or stood in the paths of sinners, or taken a seat in the band of mockers. [2] Instead his pleasure is in the law of the LORD, and in his Torah he meditates day and night. [3] And he will be like a living tree planted by streams of water, whose fruit ripens in due course, and its leaves do not fall, and all its branches that grow ripen and flourish. [4] Not so the wicked; instead, they are like the chaff that the storm-wind will drive. [5] Therefore, the wicked will not be acquitted in the great day, nor sinners in the band of the righteous, [6] Because the path of the righteous is manifest in the LORD's presence, but the paths of the wicked will perish.

Verse One

New American Standard 1995	Hebrew
[1] How blessed is the man who does not walk in the counsel of the wicked, nor stand in the path of sinners, nor sit in the seat of scoffers!	אַשְׁרֵי־הָאִישׁ אֲשֶׁר ׀ לֹא הָלַךְ 1 בַּעֲצַת רְשָׁעִים וּבְדֶרֶךְ חַטָּאִים לֹא עָמָד וּבְמוֹשַׁב לֵצִים לֹא יָשָׁב׃

Verse Analysis

אָשַׁר (*ashar*) means "moving forward toward spiritual awareness." Therefore, the term denotes that a person who wishes to learn about the LORD must move forward. The travel would allow the person to gain spiritual wealth, thus moving up the Ladder of Ascent from Malkhut to Yesod. Once in the Lower Waters of the Tree of Life, the Ruach of the person would continue in its spiritual learning to move toward the Sefirah Chesed. The spiritual walk toward Yesod is for the righteous.

The Sage Malbim said that this word applies to the spiritual attainment necessary for the World to Come. The World to Come defined by the Zohar and Kabbalah is the return of the Ruach to the Sefirah Yesod and beyond.

רָשָׁע (*rasha*) means "evildoer, or wicked." This person achieves his/her goals in life by abandoning a sense of duty and honor. This person strives for the material world and has no need or desire to learn about the spiritual world.

To move forward from the material world to the spiritual world, one has to give up wanting to gain material only and turn toward the LORD and the spiritual world. Being a part of the material world is necessary because the Ruach has to live inside the Nefesh to live in the realm of Malkhut. Therefore, being successful in acquiring material things is not bad. It is when the person's attention is solely concentrated on the material world that the person can allow their spiritual development to lag or even be ignored. The Ruach will one day leave the Nefesh. The material objects accumulated during a lifetime cannot be taken into the Lower Waters of the Tree of Life. Moving forward means to be attentive to the spiritual world and the Ruach's need to learn how to move into the realm of Yesod. According to this verse, only the persons who are attempting to increase their spiritual awareness will be permitted into the Lower Waters.

The wicked are never satisfied with their material possessions because their desire is for Nefesh instant gratification. These people want physical satisfaction above everything. This gratification works well in the material world but cannot be taken into the spiritual world. This person is not concerned with what happens to the Ruach when the Nefesh dies.

חָטָא (*chata*) means "sinner" but has the connotation of meaning a frivolous person.

This person scorns others using their materialism to avoid spiritual growth. This person does not believe in the LORD and that their power obtained everything they materially possess. This person places no gratitude for the LORD because the person does not believe in the LORD. The frivolous person takes a light-hearted approach toward the LORD and does not concern him/herself with the Mitzvot of the Torah.

The verse says that a righteous person must never take the advice of an evildoer (wicked) or a frivolous (sinner) person. The righteous person must not associate with potential enemies or scorners of the LORD's moral laws that are derived from the Scripture.

Verse Rewrite Emphasizing Spiritual Awareness

The spiritual development of a person is that he/she strides forward by avoiding the desires of the Nefesh and stands upright in following the LORD's Torah and does not say words against the LORD.

Verse Two

New American Standard 1995	Hebrew
[2] But his delight is in the law of the LORD, and in His law he meditates day and night.	כִּי אִם בְּתוֹרַת יְהֹוָה חֶפְצוֹ [2] וּבְתוֹרָתוֹ יֶהְגֶּה יוֹמָם וָלָיְלָה :

Verse Analysis

חָפֵץ (*chapetz*) means to "delight." It is the striving of a person to seek spiritually driven goals, thus increasing spiritual awareness. The night is when the materialistic part of a person can rest. In ancient days most people did not work in the evening or night. Since a person is not seeking the material world in the evening, then the person can seek out the spiritual world and spiritual awareness. The study of the Torah was usually done at night because the person would not be distracted by the demands of the material world. The day is allocated for life's tasks that are required while the Ruach resides in the Nefesh in the Sefirah Malkhut.

The Sage Hirsch said that the phrase "and in His law" or "in his Torah" did not mean the LORD's Torah but rather the personalized Torah of the student. A person wanting to increase their spiritual awareness and climb the Ladder of Ascent needs to select his/her Torah passages to be studied. This phrase means that the person must determine which passages of the Torah must be studied to learn the spiritual lesson that the LORD placed before him/her. The lesson learned will allow the person to gain righteousness and stride toward spiritual awareness and the spiritual world.

Verse Rewrite Emphasizing Spiritual Awareness

A person's spiritual awareness growth is found in the person's selection of the Torah to study, which is reviewed by night and practiced by day.

Verse Three

New American Standard 1995	Hebrew
[3] He will be like a tree *firmly* planted by streams of water, which yields its fruit in its season and its leaf does not wither; and in whatever he does, he prospers.	וְֽהָיָ֗ה כְּעֵץ֮ שָׁת֪וּל עַֽל־פַּלְגֵ֫י מָ֥יִם אֲשֶׁ֤ר פִּרְי֨וֹ ׀ יִתֵּ֬ן בְּעִתּ֗וֹ וְעָלֵ֥הוּ לֹֽא־ יִבּ֑וֹל וְכֹ֖ל אֲשֶׁר־יַעֲשֶׂ֣ה יַצְלִֽיחַ׃

Verse Analysis

שָׁת֪וּל (*shatool*) means "replanted." Young shoots of a tree are taken from the original tree and are replanted to grow new trees. When a materialistic world person becomes aware of the spiritual world, they need to be replanted. One reason is that the newfound spiritual awareness needs nourishment for the Ruach's development and character. These needs are beyond the environment of the Nefesh that the Ruach was born into. Many times this replanting must occur if the Ruach cannot find what it needs to expand and grow into the spiritual world. Sometimes this means going to a religious school or Yeshiva, or perhaps to a mentor or spiritual director.

The choice of brooks is when the person selects the best environment for study. Sometimes the first brook that is selected turns out not to be the best brook. Then the person will need to seek out a new place of study. Of course, the first place selected may be adequate until the person reaches a particular rung on the Ladder of Ascent, then a different environment may be necessary to continue the climb to Chesed.

Being replanted can mean being taken out of the material world and placed into the spiritual world. The person is planted into the material world when born. The movement to the spiritual world is the replanting of the person. Once a person moves to the spiritual world, it must always be spiritual feed.

עַל־פַּלְגֵי מָיִם (*al gal'gae mayim*) means "by streams of water" and says that there are numerous branches of study that a person can take. However, all the branches of study spring from the same source. The source is the LORD's Torah. The Torah is the source of all thinking and learning of the spiritual world.

The leaf protects the Ruach while it is developing while the fruit is the Ruach. The Torah can be considered the leaf because following the mitzvot of the Torah, the Nefesh is protected, and the Ruach can obtain spiritual nourishment.

Verse Rewrite Emphasizing Spiritual Awareness

One who becomes spiritually aware is one who has one foot in the material world and one foot in the spiritual world and draws spiritual strength from it and becomes righteous as a result of living in both worlds.

Verse Four

New American Standard 1995	Hebrew
[4] The wicked are not so, but they are like chaff which the wind drives away.	לֹא־כֵן הָרְשָׁעִים כִּי אִם־כַּמֹּץ אֲשֶׁר־תִּדְּפֶנּוּ רוּחַ :

Verse Analysis

The wicked are lawless people who are only concerned with material gains in the material world. They are not righteous in their attitudes and conducts. They do not understand that there is much more to the LORD's world than just materialism.

A grain stalk is composed of three items:

1. The kernel is for human consumption
2. The straw is for animal consumption
3. The chaff initially protects the grain but is useless when the grain matures

The chaff contained the goodness which was given to the kernel and the straw. Besides, the chaff protected the grain.

The materialistic person, when born, has goodness in them and the ability to develop spiritually but gave it up for the desires of the Nefesh. The Spirit of the LORD will destroy the person who lives only in the material world. The materialistic person had their ethical goodness removed because of their desires of the Nefesh. These are people who do not follow the mitzvot of the LORD from the Torah. The Spirit of the LORD will destroy that Ruach by disregarding it when it attempts to return to Yesod and the Lower Waters.

Verse Rewrite Emphasizing Spiritual Awareness

The materialistic person had all their ethical goodness removed, and the Spirit of the LORD disregards the person.

Verse Five

New American Standard 1995	Hebrew
⁵ Therefore the wicked will not stand in the judgment, nor sinners in the assembly of the righteous.	עַל־כֵּ֤ן ׀ לֹא־יָקֻ֣מוּ רְ֭שָׁעִים ⁵ בַּמִּשְׁפָּ֑ט וְ֝חַטָּאִ֗ים בַּעֲדַ֥ת צַדִּיקִֽים׃

Verse Analysis

מִשְׁפָּט (*mesh'fat*) means "divine judgment over the deeds of people." Judgment originates in the Sefirah Gevurah. The persons who are sinners do not repent of their sins. The LORD gives time between a sin and a punishment so that the person can recognize the sin and offer repentance. When sinners refuse to repent for their sins, the divine judgment of Gevurah will not deal with them. It means that their Ruach will not be able to return to Yesod because they are filled with unrepented sin.

רְשָׁעִים (*r'shaym*) means a person who seeks neither inner nor outer support from the LORD's moral law which has been revealed; rather these persons allow themselves to be swayed only by their passions and the environmental temptations of the material world. They will be unable to rise up or stand up at the time of divine judgment.

The Zohar says that when divine judgment occurs, the person who repented for sins and has at least performed one mitzvah throughout their life will come into the Lower Waters. The repented sins are forgotten by the LORD. At that divine time, the Accuser will come before the LORD with a list of the sins that the person had done. The LORD

18

will tell the Accuser to leave because the sins are no longer with the person because the person repented.

Verse Rewrite Emphasizing Spiritual Awareness

The people who do not believe in the LORD shall not be forgiven and will not join the righteous in the Lower Waters of the Tree of Life.

Verse Six

New American Standard 1995	Hebrew
[6] For the LORD knows the way of the righteous, but the way of the wicked will perish.	6 עַל־כֵּן ׀ לֹא־יָקֻמוּ רְשָׁעִים בַּמִּשְׁפָּט וְחַטָּאִים בַּעֲדַת צַדִּיקִים׃

Verse Analysis

The way of the righteous is that they walk their entire life following the LORD's intent for all humankind and will not allow them to perish. The Zohar says that there is at least one righteous person in all generations. The righteous persons are a reminder to the LORD that the people of the Earth need the LORD's help to change from their materialistic ways to righteous ways.

צַדִּיקִים (*tzdeekym*) means "that the righteous can be sure of their progress toward salvation because the LORD through the Shekinah will direct the righteous." The Shekinah will be available to help the righteous in their path so that when the Nefesh dies, the Ruach will be able to return to Yesod and the Lower Waters.

The people who are lawless will not receive any particular divine intervention.

Verse Rewrite Emphasizing Spiritual Awareness

For the LORD assists the righteous on their way toward salvation while the materialistic only people are doomed.

Complete Psalm Rewrite Emphasizing Spiritual Awareness

¹ The spiritual development of a person is that he/she strides forward by avoiding the desires of the Nefesh and stands upright in following the LORD's Torah and does not say words against the LORD.

² A person's spiritual awareness growth is found in the person's selection of the Torah to study, which is reviewed by night and practiced by day.

³ One who becomes spiritually aware is one who has one foot in the material world and one foot in the spiritual world and draws spiritual strength from it and becomes righteous as a result of living in both worlds.

⁴ The materialistic person had all their ethical goodness removed, and the Spirit of the LORD disregards the person.

⁵ The people who do not believe in the LORD shall not be forgiven and will not join the righteous in the Lower Waters of the Tree of Life.

⁶ For the LORD assists the righteous on their way toward salvation while the materialistic only people are doomed.

Lessons from the Psalm

1. The return of the Ruach to join its soul mate is imperative
2. People need to learn the ways of the Torah
3. To please the LORD, a person must follow the mitzvot

Definitions

Zohar - "The Zohar (Hebrew זֹהַר; Splendor, radiance) is widely considered the most important work of Kabbalah, Jewish mysticism. It is a mystical commentary on the Torah (five books of Moses), written in medieval Aramaic and medieval Hebrew. It contains a mystical discussion of the nature of God, the origin and structure of the universe, the nature of souls, sin, redemption, good and evil, and related topics. The Zohar is not one book, but a group of books. These books include scriptural interpretations as well as material on theosophic theology, mythical cosmogony, mystical psychology, and what some would call anthropology." Source: https://www.jewishvirtuallibrary.org/the-zohar

Kabbalah – "Kabbalah (also spelled Kabalah, Cabala, Qabala)—sometimes translated as "mysticism" or "occult knowledge—is a part of Jewish tradition that deals with the essence of God. Whether it entails a sacred text, an experience, or the way things work, Kabbalists believe that God moves in mysterious ways. However, Kabbalists also believe that true knowledge and understanding of that inner, mysterious process is obtainable, and through that knowledge, the greatest intimacy with God can be attained." Source: https://reformjudaism.org/what-kabbalah

The Tree of Life

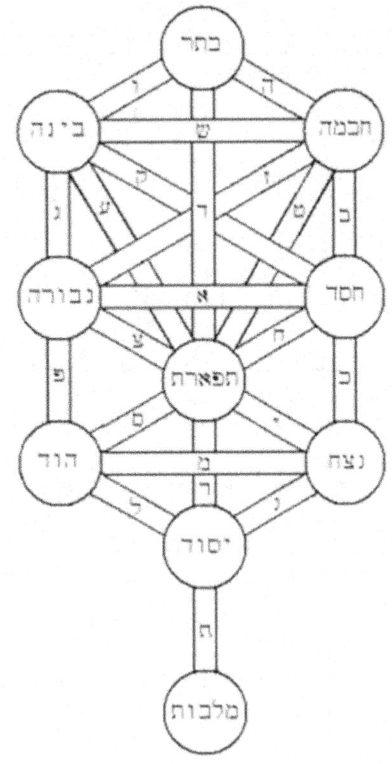

"**Isaac ben Solomon Luria**, byname **Ha-ari** (Hebrew: The Lion**)**, (born 1534, Jerusalem, Palestine, Ottoman Empire—died August 5, 1572, Safed, Syria [now Zefat, Israel]), eponymous founder of the Lurianic school of Kabbala (Jewish esoteric mysticism). Source: https://www.britannica.com/biography/Isaac-ben-Solomon-Luria

Samson Hirsch - It has often been said that Orthodox Judaism has always existed since the Jews received the Torah on Mt. Sinai and that Conservative Judaism was a reaction to Reform Judaism, however, that is not entirely accurate. In fact, modern Orthodoxy did not exist until the reforms and innovations of Rabbi Samson Raphael Hirsch.

Hirsch was born in 1808 in Hamburg, Germany. He went to the public schools, where he was strongly influenced by Schiller and Hegel, and received his Jewish education at home. His father was an observant Jew. His grandfather, Mendel Frankfurter, was the founder of the Talmud Torah in Hamburg. Through the education of his teachers, considered German Jewry's greatest Talmudists, who were proficient in both non-Jewish and Jewish culture, Hirsch decided to train for the rabbinate with the aim of demonstrating that traditional Judaism and Western culture are compatible with each other. From 1823 to 1829 he studied under Rabbi Jacob Ettlinger, a distinguished German Jewish Talmudist. He than entered the University of Bonn. While at Bonn one of his classmates was Abraham Geiger, who later became a leader of the Reform movement. At Bonn, he studied classical languages, history and philosophy. Source: https://www.jewishvirtuallibrary.org/samson-raphael-hirsch

Sefer Yetzirah "(Hebrew: ספר יצירה *Sēpher Yəṣîrâh*, *Book of Formation*, or *Book of Creation*) is the title of the earliest extant book on Jewish mysticism, although some early commentators treated it as a treatise on mathematical and linguistic theory as opposed to Kabbalah. *Yetzirah* is more literally translated as "Formation"; the word *Briah* is used for "Creation". The book is traditionally ascribed to the patriarch Abraham, although others attribute its writing to Rabbi Akiva. Modern scholars have not reached consensus on the question of its origins. According to Rabbi Saadia Gaon, the objective of the book's author was to convey in writing how the things of our universe came into existence.

The famous opening words of the book are as follows:

By thirty-two mysterious paths of wisdom Jah has engraved [all things], [who is] the Lord of hosts, the God of Israel, the living God, the Almighty God, He that is uplifted and exalted, He that Dwells forever, and whose Name is holy; having created His world by three [derivatives] of [the Hebrew root-word] *sᵉfr*: namely, *sefer* (a book), *sefor* (a count) and *sippur* (a story), along with ten calibrations of empty space, twenty-two letters [of the Hebrew alphabet], [of which] three are principal [letters] (i.e. א מ ש), seven are double-sounding [consonants] (i.e. בג״ד כפר״ת) and twelve are ordinary [letters] (i.e. ה ו ז ח ט י ל נ ס ע צ ק).” Source: https://en.wikipedia.org/wiki/Sefer_Yetzirah

PSALM TWO

Language

New American Standard 1995	Hebrew
[1] Why are the nations in an uproar and the peoples devising a vain thing? [2] The kings of the earth take their stand and the rulers take counsel together against the LORD and against His Anointed, saying, [3] "Let us tear their fetters apart and cast away their cords from us!" [4] He who sits in the heavens laughs, the Lord scoffs at them. [5] Then He will speak to them in His anger and terrify them in His fury, saying, [6] "But as for Me, I have installed My King Upon Zion, My holy mountain." [7] "I will surely tell of the decree of the LORD: He said to Me, 'You are My Son, today I have begotten You. [8] 'Ask of Me, and I will surely give the nations as Your inheritance, and the *very* ends of the earth as Your possession. [9] 'You shall break them with a rod of iron, you shall shatter them like earthenware.'" [10] Now therefore, O kings, show discernment; take warning, O judges of the earth. [11] Worship the LORD with reverence and rejoice with trembling. [12] Do homage to the Son, that He not become angry, and you perish *in* the way, for His wrath may soon be kindled. How blessed are all who take refuge in Him!	לָמָּה רָגְשׁוּ גוֹיִם וּלְאֻמִּים יֶהְגּוּ־רִיק ׃ ² יִתְיַצְּבוּ ׀ מַלְכֵי־אֶרֶץ וְרוֹזְנִים נוֹסְדוּ־יָחַד עַל־יְהוָה וְעַל־מְשִׁיחוֹ ׃ ³ נְנַתְּקָה אֶת־מוֹסְרוֹתֵימוֹ וְנַשְׁלִיכָה מִמֶּנּוּ עֲבֹתֵימוֹ ׃ ⁴ יוֹשֵׁב בַּשָּׁמַיִם יִשְׂחָק אֲדֹנָי יִלְעַג־לָמוֹ ׃ ⁵ אָז יְדַבֵּר אֵלֵימוֹ בְאַפּוֹ וּבַחֲרוֹנוֹ יְבַהֲלֵמוֹ ׃ ⁶ וַאֲנִי נָסַכְתִּי מַלְכִּי עַל־צִיּוֹן הַר־קָדְשִׁי ׃ ⁷ אֲסַפְּרָה אֶל חֹק יְהוָה אָמַר אֵלַי בְּנִי אַתָּה אֲנִי הַיּוֹם יְלִדְתִּיךָ ׃ ⁸ שְׁאַל מִמֶּנִּי וְאֶתְּנָה גוֹיִם נַחֲלָתֶךָ וַאֲחֻזָּתְךָ אַפְסֵי־אָרֶץ ׃ ⁹ תְּרֹעֵם בְּשֵׁבֶט בַּרְזֶל כִּכְלִי יוֹצֵר תְּנַפְּצֵם ׃ ¹⁰ וְעַתָּה מְלָכִים הַשְׂכִּילוּ הִוָּסְרוּ שֹׁפְטֵי אָרֶץ ׃ ¹¹ עִבְדוּ אֶת־יְהוָה בְּיִרְאָה וְגִילוּ בִּרְעָדָה ׃ ¹² נַשְּׁקוּ־בַר פֶּן־יֶאֱנַף ׀ וְתֹאבְדוּ דֶרֶךְ כִּי־יִבְעַר כִּמְעַט אַפּוֹ אַשְׁרֵי כָּל־חוֹסֵי בוֹ ׃

Targum

[1] Why are the Gentiles disturbed, and the nations murmuring vanity? [2] The kings of the earth arise and the rulers will join together to rebel in the LORD's presence, and to strive against his Anointed. [3] They say, "Let us break their bonds, and let us throw off their chains from us." [4] The one who sits in heaven will laugh; the word of the LORD will mock at them. [5] Then he will speak to them in his strength, and in his wrath he will frighten them. [6] I have anointed my king, and appointed him over my sanctuary. [7] I will tell of the covenant of the LORD. He said: "You are as dear to me as a son to a father (abba), pure as if this day I had created you." [8] Ask me and I will give the riches of the Gentiles as your inheritance, the rulers of the ends of the earth as your holding. [9] You will shatter them as with a rod of iron, like a potter's vessel you will break them. [10] And now, O kings, grow wise; accept discipline, O princes of the earth. [11] Worship in the presence of the LORD with fear, and pray with trembling. [12] Accept instruction lest he be angry, and you lose your way; for his wrath will tarry a little. Happy all who trust in his word!

Verse One and Two

New American Standard 1995	Hebrew
[1] Why are the nations in an uproar and the peoples devising a vain thing? [2] The kings of the earth take their stand and the rulers take counsel together against the LORD and against His Anointed, saying,	לָ֤מָּה רָגְשׁ֣וּ גוֹיִ֑ם וּלְאֻמִּ֗ים יֶהְגּוּ־רִֽיק׃ יִֽתְיַצְּב֨וּ ׀ מַלְכֵי־אֶ֗רֶץ וְרוֹזְנִ֥ים נֽוֹסְדוּ־יָ֑חַד עַל־יְ֝הוָה וְעַל־מְשִׁיחֽוֹ׃

Verse Analysis

The life of a nation is tied to the life of the individuals who live in said nations. The people must want spiritual awareness in order to survive. The people and leaders need legal obedience to moral laws. Only through ethical and moral endeavors can the nations of the world be assured of the LORD's help.

Corruption by materialistic leaders will destroy a nation. It is best to have leaders who have one foot in the material world and the other foot in the spiritual world.

לָמָּה (lama) – means "why." Why is it important to be morally righteous? Only the morally righteous can be sure of aid and a future by following the LORD's sovereign rule.

רָגַשׁ (rag' sh) – means "to put in motion by some outside influence." This Psalm refers to the time when King David had solidified the kingdom. After King Saul's death his remaining sons attempted to take the throne of Israel. A civil war broke out for seven years. King David won the civil war and was putting the kingdom back together. The Philistines did not want David to have a strong Israel and prepared to attack them.

מְשִׁיחוֹ (m' sheecho) – means "anointed one." King David was anointed by the prophet Samuel for the LORD's house and the moral future of all mankind. The line of David produced Solomon, who built the LORD's house and Jesus the Messiah.

Verse Rewrite Emphasizing Spiritual Awareness

Why does the material driven Philistines gather to attack Israel? (v. 1)
Their king called an army together in secret to attack the LORD's people (Israel) and the LORD's King (David). (v. 2)

Verse Three

New American Standard 1995	Hebrew
[3] "Let us tear their fetters apart and cast away their cords from us!"	נְֽנַתְּקָה אֶת־מֽוֹסְרֽוֹתֵימוֹ וְנַשְׁלִיכָה מִמֶּנּוּ עֲבֹתֵֽימוֹ׃

Verse Analysis

נְֽנַתְּקָה (n'nat'cha) - means "to forcibly separate, to tear asunder." King David had created agreements between the tribes to work together as a nation. The survival of Israel depended upon the twelve tribes coming together to become one nation. If the tribes did not come together to form a nation, the individual tribes would have been picked off one by one. A central army needed to be created to fight any of the surrounding nations from attacking Israel. The book of Judges describes the time when the individual tribes were separate. During that time period, the surrounding nations attacked the different tribes. King David's army was able to establish a strong kingdom, and he expanded the territory of Israel.

עֲבֹת (avot) — means "a cord of which the forces of activity are harnessed." It infers the cords of a yoke (agreements to protect one another) between the various tribes, which created the nation of Israel. The cords that David created were spiritual. He told the people that they needed to remain loyal to the LORD, who brought them out of Egypt. The spiritual connection needed to be established between the tribes to create the nation.

Verse Rewrite Emphasizing Spiritual Awareness

The Philistines wanted to cut the spiritual cords between the people of Israel and the LORD.

Verse Four

New American Standard 1995	Hebrew
⁴ He who sits in the heavens laughs, the Lord scoffs at them.	יוֹשֵׁב בַּשָּׁמַיִם יִשְׂחָק אֲדֹנָי יִלְעַג־לָמוֹ׃

Verse Analysis

יָשַׁב (yasha) – means "to sit, remain, dwell." The LORD permits men to engage in lengthy experiments in the carrying out of their plans. He allows materialistically minded people to gather their earthly treasures hoping people will see the need for the spiritual world.

אֲדֹנָי (adonai) – means "my master." A person who refers to the LORD as Adonai is dedicated to serving the LORD. This person works for His purpose, wanting to learn about the spiritual world.

The LORD mocks people who are only interested in the material world.

Verse Rewrite Emphasizing Spiritual Awareness

The LORD in Heaven laughs at people who are only interested in the material world, like the Philistines.

New American Standard 1995	Hebrew
[5] Then He will speak to them in His anger and terrify them in His fury, saying,	אָז יְדַבֵּר אֵלֵימוֹ בְאַפּוֹ וּבַחֲרוֹנוֹ יְבַהֲלֵמוֹ ׃

Verse Analysis

אָז יְדַבֵּר (atz y' dabar) – means "to seek enduring salvation without paying homage to the moral law."

The LORD is a free, moral, and personal God who rules over the material and physical world. The LORD hears the vain words of the earthly-minded Kings who are only interested in material conquests and is saddened that they have no interested in the spiritual world

Verse Rewrite Emphasizing Spiritual Awareness

The LORD hears the words of the Philistine king and responds to him in a way that terrifies the king's nation.

Verse Six

New American Standard 1995	Hebrew
[6] "But as for Me, I have installed My King Upon Zion, My holy mountain."	וַאֲנִי נָסַכְתִּי מַלְכִּי עַל־צִיּוֹן הַר־קָדְשִׁי׃

Verse Analysis

Jerusalem was a place on Earth that allows positive energy from the Right Column of the Tree of Life to enter Malkhut. The Zohar says that there are several places on the Earth where the positive energy of the right column can enter Malkhut. Also, several places on Earth allow the negative energy of the left column to enter. Unfortunately, the accumulation of negative energy in a specific place causes the Klippot of Evil Inclination to form.

The LORD had David anointed by Samuel to lead the LORD's people into the spiritual world. The LORD would not allow the Philistines to remove David as the King because he was chosen by the LORD and not by the people.

Verse Rewrite Emphasizing Spiritual Awareness

The LORD anointed David because he could lead the people in their spiritual journey from the positive energy of Zion.

Verse Seven

New American Standard 1995	Hebrew
[7] "I will surely tell of the decree of the LORD: He said to Me, 'You are My Son, today I have begotten You.	אֲסַפְּרָה אֶל חֹק יְהוָה אָמַר אֵלַי בְּנִי אַתָּה אֲנִי הַיּוֹם יְלִדְתִּיךָ :

Verse Analysis

אֲסַפְּרָה אֶל חֹק (asaf'ra el chok) means "recounting of facts with a movement toward a goal."

David was to be the spiritual light by being the righteous person of his generation. The Zohar says that there is at least one righteous person in every generation. King David was the righteous person of his generation. It was through the righteous that the LORD could send His Light to the people of the world.

"You are my son" means that David became the King because of the LORD's actions, not by the election of men. The LORD chose David because he desired to serve the LORD.

David's selection as a spiritual leader was something new that the LORD had done.

Verse Rewrite Emphasizing Spiritual Awareness

David was obligated to proclaim: the LORD told him that he was selected by the LORD, not by humans, to lead the LORD's people to the spiritual world.

Verse Eight

New American Standard 1995	Hebrew
[8] Ask me and I will give the riches of the Gentiles as your inheritance, the rulers of the ends of the earth as your holding.	שְׁאַל מִמֶּנִּי וְאֶתְּנָה גוֹיִם נַחֲלָתֶךָ וַאֲחֻזָּתְךָ אַפְסֵי־אָרֶץ׃

Verse Analysis

The LORD told David to gird himself with purity, and so the people of the Earth would move forward toward the spiritual world. The inheritance is to cure the nations of the world of materialism. The will of the LORD can be done once the materialism of the Nefesh is removed.

Verse Rewrite Emphasizing Spiritual Awareness

The LORD offered David the entire world so he could teach the people the ways of the LORD.

Verse Nine

New American Standard 1995	Hebrew
9 'You shall break them with a rod of iron, you shall shatter them like earthenware.'"	תְּרֹעֵם בְּשֵׁבֶט בַּרְזֶל כִּכְלִי יוֹצֵר תְּנַפְּצֵם :

Verse Analysis

The LORD instructed David that he should pray that the nations that surround his kingdom will submit to the spiritual light and ethical demands that he will bring them. When David conquered a nation, he brought the Light of Ein Sof with him. He was to teach them about the LORD. David's teaching would spread the Torah, thus the LORD's Will, throughout the world. Any nation that decided to stay in the material world would be destroyed. Materialistic nations tend to fight other nations or themselves to gain more material wealth. Many times the fighting destroys the nation.

Verse Rewrite Emphasizing Spiritual Awareness

Any nation rising against David will be destroyed.

Verse Ten

New American Standard 1995	Hebrew
[10] Now therefore, O kings, show discernment; take warning, O judges of the earth.	וְעַתָּה מְלָכִים הַשְׂכִּילוּ הִוָּסְרוּ שֹׁפְטֵי אָרֶץ׃

Verse Analysis

וְעַתָּה (v'ata) – means "and now." The LORD proclaimed the His design for Malkhut. Therefore, it must be implemented, comprehended, and understood by the people in Malkhut.

הַשְׂכִּילוּ (has'keylou) – means "comprehend this."

שֹׁפְטֵי אָרֶץ (shof'tai aretz) – means "to act as a law giver."

Verse Rewrite Emphasizing Spiritual Awareness

Kings and judges of the Earth must learn about the spiritual world.

Verse Eleven

New American Standard 1995	Hebrew
[11] Worship the LORD with reverence and rejoice with trembling.	עִבְדוּ אֶת־יְהוָה בְּיִרְאָה וְגִילוּ בִּרְעָדָה:

Verse Analysis

עִבְדוּ (ev' do) – means "consecrate yourself to the service of the LORD." The spiritual world needs to be brought to the people in Malkhut. It is difficult for people who are prosperous materialistically to understand that there is more to the world than material wealth. Materialism is necessary because the Sefirah Malkhut is a physically based Sefirah. However, the spiritual world of Yesod and the Upper World is critical for the Ruach to comprehend before the death of the Nefesh. David's role was to bring that understanding. Paying reverence to the LORD is the understanding that there is a spiritual world and the need to be a part of it. Trembling is a physical response of the Light of Ein Sof, which is overwhelming to those who are new to the experience.

וְגִילוּ בִּרְעָדָה: (v'geelou beer' ada) means "greatest joy, most joyous emotion." With great joy, one accepts the spiritual world that the LORD has created for our Ruach to return to. The Lower Waters of the Tree of Life is where our image of the LORD resides. The Ruach must be taught about the spiritual world. It is joyous to be able to live in Malkhut and keep all of the LORD's laws.

Verse Rewrite Emphasizing Spiritual Awareness

Remember that while rejoicing, one must revere the LORD so that no Law is broken.

Verse Twelve

New American Standard 1995	Hebrew
[12] Do homage to the Son, that He not become angry, and you perish *in* the way, for His wrath may soon be kindled. How blessed are all who take refuge in Him!	נַשְּׁקוּ־בַר פֶּן־יֶאֱנַף וְתֹאבְדוּ דֶרֶךְ כִּי־יִבְעַר כִּמְעַט אַפּוֹ אַשְׁרֵי כָּל־ חוֹסֵי בוֹ

Verse Analysis

The path of lawless persons leads to destruction and will eventually disappear. A goal of life is to return to Yesod. Therefore, stride forward toward salvation by trusting the LORD and always asking for His help. King David never forgot that the LORD placed him on the throne of Israel. He always asked for the LORD's help through his prayers. People today should be doing the same thing.

Verse Rewrite Emphasizing Spiritual Awareness

Yearn for the way of the spiritual world because any other path leads to doom and the anger of the LORD. Praise the LORD always and place your trust in Him, and He will show you the path to the spiritual world.

Complete Psalm Rewrite Emphasizing Spiritual Awareness

[1] Why does the material driven Philistines gather to attack Israel?

2 Their king called an army together in secret to attack the LORD's people (Israel) and the LORD's King (David).

[3] The Philistines wanted to cut the spiritual cords between the people of Israel and the LORD.

[4] The LORD in Heaven laughs at people who are only interested in the material world, like the Philistines.

[5] The LORD hears the words of the Philistine king and responds to him in a way that terrifies the king's nation.

[6] The LORD anointed David because he could lead the people in their spiritual journey from the positive energy of Zion.

[7] David was obligated to proclaim: the LORD told him that he was selected by the LORD, not by humans, to lead the LORD's people to the spiritual world.

[8] The LORD offered David the entire world so he could teach the people the ways of the LORD.

[9] Any nation rising against David will be destroyed.

[10] Kings and judges of the Earth must learn about the spiritual world.

[11] Remember that while rejoicing, one must revere the LORD so that no Law is broken.

[12] Yearn for the way of the spiritual world because any other path leads to doom and the anger of the LORD. Praise the LORD always and place your trust in Him, and He will show you the path to the spiritual world.

PSALM THREE

Language

<table>
<tr><th>New American Standard 1995</th><th>Hebrew</th></tr>
<tr><td>

A Psalm of David, when he fled from Absalom his son.

¹ O LORD, how my adversaries have increased! Many are rising up against me.

² Many are saying of my soul, "There is no deliverance for him in God." Selah.

³ But You, O LORD, are a shield about me, my glory, and the One who lifts my head.

⁴ I was crying to the LORD with my voice, and He answered me from His holy mountain. Selah.

⁵ I lay down and slept; I awoke, for the LORD sustains me.

⁶ I will not be afraid of ten thousands of people who have set themselves against me round about.

⁷ Arise, O LORD; save me, O my God! For You have smitten all my enemies on the cheek; You have shattered the teeth of the wicked.

⁸ Salvation belongs to the LORD; Your blessing *be* upon Your people! Selah.

</td><td>

מִזְמוֹר לְדָוִד בְּבָרְחוֹ מִפְּנֵי |
אַבְשָׁלוֹם בְּנוֹ׃ ² יְהוָה מָה־רַבּוּ צָרָי
רַבִּים קָמִים עָלָי׃ ³ רַבִּים אֹמְרִים
לְנַפְשִׁי אֵין יְשׁוּעָתָה לּוֹ בֵאלֹהִים
סֶלָה׃ ⁴ וְאַתָּה יְהוָה מָגֵן בַּעֲדִי
כְּבוֹדִי וּמֵרִים רֹאשִׁי׃ ⁵ קוֹלִי אֶל־
יְהוָה אֶקְרָא וַיַּעֲנֵנִי מֵהַר קָדְשׁוֹ
סֶלָה׃ ⁶ אֲנִי שָׁכַבְתִּי וָאִישָׁנָה
הֱקִיצוֹתִי כִּי יְהוָה יִסְמְכֵנִי׃ ⁷ לֹא־
אִירָא מֵרִבְבוֹת עָם אֲשֶׁר סָבִיב
שָׁתוּ עָלָי׃ ⁸ קוּמָה יְהוָה | הוֹשִׁיעֵנִי
אֱלֹהַי כִּי־הִכִּיתָ אֶת־כָּל־אֹיְבַי לֶחִי
שִׁנֵּי רְשָׁעִים שִׁבַּרְתָּ׃ ⁹ לַיהוָה
הַיְשׁוּעָה עַל־עַמְּךָ בִרְכָתֶךָ סֶּלָה׃

</td></tr>
</table>

Targum

¹ A psalm of David, when he fled from the presence of Absalom his son. ² O LORD, how many are my oppressors, many who arise against me. ³ Many say to my soul, "There is no redemption for him in God forever." ⁴ But you, O LORD, are a shield over me, my glory and the one who raises my head. ⁵ I pray [with] my voice in the presence of the LORD; he will accept my prayer from the mount of his sanctuary forever. ⁶ I lay down, and I slept; I awoke, because the LORD sustains me. ⁷ I will not be afraid of the strife of people who have gathered against me all around. ⁸ Arise, O LORD, redeem me, O my God; for you have struck all my enemies on their cheek, you have broken the teeth of the wicked. ⁹ Redemption is from the presence of the LORD; your blessings are to your people forever.

Interlinear

O   Lord   how   my   adversaries   have   increased
יהוה   מָה   צָר   רָבַב
yhwh   mah   tzar   ravav

Many   are   rising   up   against   me
רַב   קוּם   עַל
rav   qum   ʿal

Psa. 3:2   Many   are   saying   of   my   soul
Lex   רַב   אָמַר   נֶפֶשׁ
Lex Trl   rav   ʾamar   nefesh

There   is   no   deliverance   for   him   in
אֵין   אֵין   יְשׁוּעָה
ʾayin   ʾayin   yeshuʿah

God   Selah
אֱלֹהִים   סֶלָה
ʾelohim   selah

Psa. 3:3   But   You   O   Lord   are   a   shield
Lex   יהוה   מָגֵן
Lex Trl   yhwh   magen

about   me   My   glory   and   the   One   who   lifts   my
בַּעַד   כָּבוֹד   רוּם
baʿad   kavod   rum

head
רֹאשׁ
roʾsh

Psa. 3:4   I   was   crying   to   the   Lord   with   my   voice
Lex   קָרָא   יהוה   קוֹל
Lex Trl   qaraʾ   yhwh   qol

And He answered me from His holy mountain
עָנָה   קֹדֶשׁ   הַר
ʿanah   qodesh   har

Selah
סֶלָה
selah

Psa. 3:5	I	lay	down	and	slept
Lex		שָׁכַב	שָׁכַב		יָשֵׁן
Lex Trl		shakhav	shakhav		yashen

	I	awoke	for	the	Lord	sustains	me
Lex		קִיץ			יהוה	סָמַךְ	
Lex Trl		qitz			yhwh	samakh	

Psa. 3:6	I	will	not	be	afraid	of	ten	thousands	of	people
Lex					יָרֵא		רְבָבָה	רְבָבָה		עַם
Lex Trl					yareʾ		revavah	revavah		ʿam

	Who	have	set	themselves	against	me	round
Lex	אֲשֶׁר		שִׁית		עַל		סָבִיב
Lex Trl	ʾasher		shit		ʿal		saviv

about
סָבִיב
saviv

Psa. 3:7	Arise	O	Lord
Lex	קוּם		יהוה
Lex Trl	qum		yhwh

	save	me	O	my	God	For	You	have
Lex	יָשַׁע				אֱלֹהִים			
Lex Trl	yashaʿ				ʾelohim			

	smitten	all	my	enemies	on	the	cheek	You
Lex	נָכָה	כֹּל		אָיַב			לְחִי	
Lex Trl	nakhah	kol		ʾayav			lechi	

	have	shattered	the	teeth	of	the	wicked

שָׁבַר
shavar

שֵׁן
shen

רָשָׁע
rashaʿ

Psa. 3:8   Salvation   belongs   to   the   Lord
Lex   יְשׁוּעָה   יהוה
Lex Trl   yeshuʿah   yhwh

Your   blessing   be   upon   Your   people
בְּרָכָה   עַם
berakhah   ʿam

Selah
סֶלָה
selah

Superscript

New American Standard 1995	Hebrew
A Psalm of David, when he fled from Absalom his son.	מִזְמוֹר לְדָוִד בְּבָרְחוֹ מִפְּנֵי אַבְשָׁלוֹם בְּנוֹ ׃

Superscript Analysis

Psalm One and two tell the story of the glory of King David. It is interesting that when the book of Psalms was put together, this Psalm became Psalm three. This Psalm talks about the punishment from Gevurah concerning David's immoral affair with Bathsheba. When word got out about David's sin, his firstborn son Absalom decided to lead a revolt to remove David from the throne of Israel. There were plenty of David haters who went along with Absalom. David's sin caused him to lose the gains that he had made on the Ladder of Ascent. David backslid because his Nefesh was strong enough that it caused him to want what the material world offered. The Nefesh is sometimes difficult to control. Psalm three demonstrates that humans are not perfect – there is no superhuman perfection.

Whenever the name David occurs before the phrase "a song," divine inspiration comes first. When "a song" is before the name of "David," it means that David elevated himself to the level of holy exultation because of his Psalm.

In this Psalm, David put himself in front of the LORD for judgment. He appealed to the Sefirot Gevurah for judgment, punishment, and forgiveness of his sin.

Superscript Rewrite Emphasizing Spiritual Awareness

A song of David as he fled from his son Absolom. David placed himself before Gevurah for judgment and viewed Absalom's revolt as a part of his punishment.

Verse One

New American Standard 1995	Hebrew
[1] O LORD, how my adversaries have increased! Many are rising up against me.	יְהוָה מָה־רַבּוּ צָרָי רַבִּים קָמִים עָלָי׃

Verse Analysis

The Absalom revolt was a part of David's atonement for his double sin. The first sin was adultery. The second sin was premeditated murder. The oppressors are the people who were against David and joined Absalom during the revolt.

Verse Rewrite Emphasizing Spiritual Awareness

LORD, how many of my political enemies have joined Absalom in his revolt.

Verse Two

New American Standard 1995	Hebrew
[2] Many are saying of my soul, "There is no deliverance for him in God." Selah.	רַבִּים אֹמְרִים לְנַפְשִׁי אֵין יְשׁוּעָתָה לּוֹ בֵאלֹהִים סֶלָה׃

Verse Analysis

The soul is considered the Nefesh, Ruach, and Neshamah. David turned to the Sefirah Gevurah for help. David knew that judgment had to come to him. By pleading to Gevurah, he received judgment and punishment immediately. He did hope that Chesed would be able to shine mercy on him. If not, he was ready to accept Gevurah's punishment for his sins.

The people of Israel believed that David would not receive help from the LORD. But David's appeal to Gevurah did bring him forgiveness. The Sefirah Gevurah can give judgment while punishing him.

Selah, at the end of a verse, is there to tell the reader that he/she should pause and meditate on the verse.

Verse Rewrite Emphasizing Spiritual Awareness

The people of Israel did not believe that the Sefirah Gevurah would forgive David because David's two sins required the death punishment, according to the Torah.

Verse Three

New American Standard 1995	Hebrew
[3] But You, O LORD, are a shield about me, my glory, and the One who lifts my head.	רַבִּים אֹמְרִים לְנַפְשִׁי אֵין יְשׁוּעָתָה לּוֹ בֵאלֹהִים סֶלָה:

Verse Analysis

David believed that the Sefirah Chesed would shine love and mercy on him even during a time of Gevurah's judgment. David's chastisement was intended to guide him to a better future. It also brought him back to understanding that he needed to control the urges of his Nefesh. There is the hope of forgiveness for all sinners.

Verse Rewrite Emphasizing Spiritual Awareness

Chesed was with David even after his sin, and he knew that he would be restored in both the material and the spiritual world. He would be allowed to reclimb the Ladder of Ascent.

Verse Four

New American Standard 1995	Hebrew
[4] I was crying to the LORD with my voice, and He answered me from His holy mountain. Selah.	וָאֶקְרָא יְהוָה קוֹלִי אֶקְרָא וַיַּעֲנֵנִי מֵהַר קָדְשׁוֹ סֶלָה׃

Verse Analysis

David believed that if the LORD heard his voice while weeping, then it will be the LORD whom he was calling.

Verse Rewrite Emphasizing Spiritual Awareness

The LORD knows my cry for help before I say it because I cried on the holy mountain of Zion. (Pause and meditate on this verse.)

New American Standard 1995	Hebrew
[5] I lay down and slept; I awoke, for the LORD sustains me.	קוֹלִי אֶל־יְהוָה אֶקְרָא וַיַּעֲנֵנִי מֵהַר קָדְשׁוֹ סֶלָה:

Verse Analysis

אֲנִי שָׁכַבְתִּי (ani shachav'tea) – connotatively means "I take the assurance that the LORD has heard me." David was confident that the LORD would hear his prayers.

שָׁכַב (shacar) definitions:
1. lie down
    a. prostrated
    b. to sleep,
    c. lie on
    d. lie
    e. lie, of lamb
2. lodge (for the night)
3. of sexual relations

David never panicked because he always felt the Shekinah was with him. The Shekinah led David on his way when he fled from Absalom. David placed his trust in the Shekinah to lead him to the green pastures.

Verse Rewrite Emphasizing Spiritual Awareness

David was able to sleep through the night because he knew the Shekinah would protect him.

Verse Six

New American Standard 1995	Hebrew
⁶ I will not be afraid of ten thousands of people who have set themselves against me round about.	אֲנִי שָׁכַבְתִּי וָאִישָׁנָה הֱקִיצוֹתִי כִּי יְהוָה יִסְמְכֵנִי׃

Verse Analysis

רְבָבָה (r' vava) – means "multitude, myriad, ten thousand." Generally, in David's day, anything over one thousand was considered a significant amount. Therefore, any number of over one thousand is a good translation. The Targum does not offer a number.

Verse Rewrite Emphasizing Spiritual Awareness

David's confidence in the LORD was strong that he did not fear Absalom.

Verse Seven

New American Standard 1995	Hebrew
[7] Arise, O LORD; save me, O my God! For You have smitten all my enemies on the cheek; You have shattered the teeth of the wicked.	קוּמָה יְהוָה ׀ הוֹשִׁיעֵנִי אֱלֹהַי כִּי־ הִכִּיתָ אֶת־כָּל־אֹיְבַי לֶחִי שִׁנֵּי רְשָׁעִים שִׁבַּרְתָּ

Verse Analysis

Gevurah pronounced judgment over David's foes before they revolted because David was the LORD's anointed. Gevruah was not going to allow an enemy of David to remove him from the throne. Therefore, it can be said that the enemy of David was an enemy of the LORD. David's foes violated the Torah by attacking him.

Materialistic people violate the Torah because they are either ignorant of the spiritual world or do not want to be a part of it. David's enemies wanted the material gains of overthrowing the standing government.

Verse Rewrite Emphasizing Spiritual Awareness

Rise LORD and save David because Gevurah already judges his enemies as wicked.

Verse Eight

New American Standard 1995	Hebrew
Salvation belongs to the LORD; Your blessing *be* upon Your people! Selah.	לַיהוָה הַיְשׁוּעָה עַל־עַמְּךָ בִרְכָתֶךָ סֶּלָה׃

Verse Analysis

This verse is the reflective recantation of the call to Gevurah over his enemies, which David mentioned in verse seven. David concluded the Psalm by saying that the experience with Absalom taught him a lesson about allowing the Nefesh to take control of his soul.

Verse Rewrite Emphasizing Spiritual Awareness

The LORD granted victory to His people with His blessings through the Shekinah. (Pause and meditate on this verse.)

Complete Psalm Rewrite Emphasizing Spiritual Awareness

A song of David as he fled from his son Absolom. David placed himself before Gevurah for judgment and viewed Absalom's revolt as a part of his punishment.

[1] LORD, how many of my political enemies have joined Absalom in his revolt.

[2] The people of Israel did not believe that the Sefirah Gevurah would forgive David because David's two sins required the death punishment, according to the Torah.

[3] Chesed was with David even after his sin, and he knew that he would be restored in both the material and the spiritual world. He would be allowed to reclimb the Ladder of Ascent.

[4] The LORD knows my cry for help before I say it because I cried on the holy mountain of Zion. (Pause and meditate on this verse.)

[5] David was able to sleep through the night because he knew the Shekinah would protect him.

[6] David's confidence in the LORD was strong that he did not fear Absalom.

[7] Rise LORD and save David because Gevurah already judges his enemies as wicked.

[8] The LORD granted victory to His people with His blessings through the Shekinah. (Pause and meditate on this verse.)

Lanugage

New American Standard 1995	Hebrew
Psa. 4:0 For the choir director; on stringed instruments. A Psalm of David. **Psa. 4:1** Answer me when I call, O God of my righteousness! You have relieved me in my distress; Be gracious to me and hear my prayer. **Psa. 4:2** O sons of men, how long will my honor become a reproach? *How long* will you love what is worthless and aim at deception? Selah. ³ But know that the LORD has set apart the godly man for Himself; The LORD hears when I call to Him. **Psa. 4:4** Tremble, and do not sin; Meditate in your heart upon your bed, and be still. Selah. ⁵ Offer the sacrifices of righteousness, And trust in the LORD. **Psa. 4:6** Many are saying, "*Who will show us *any* good?" Lift up the light of Your countenance upon us, O LORD! ⁷ You have put gladness in my heart, More than when their grain and new wine abound. ⁸ In peace I will both lie down and sleep, For You alone, O LORD, make me to dwell in safety.	‫לַמְנַצֵּחַ בִּנְגִינוֹת מִזְמוֹר לְדָוִד ׃ ²‬ ‫בְּקָרְאִי עֲנֵנִי ׀ אֱלֹהֵי צִדְקִי בַּצָּר‬ ‫הִרְחַבְתָּ לִּי חָנֵּנִי וּשְׁמַע תְּפִלָּתִי ׃ ³‬ ‫בְּנֵי אִישׁ עַד־מֶה כְבוֹדִי לִכְלִמָּה‬ ‫תֶּאֱהָבוּן רִיק תְּבַקְשׁוּ כָזָב סֶלָה ׃ ⁴‬ ‫וּדְעוּ כִּי־הִפְלָה יְהוָה חָסִיד לוֹ‬ ‫יְהוָה יִשְׁמַע בְּקָרְאִי אֵלָיו ׃ ⁵ רִגְזוּ‬ ‫וְאַל־תֶּחֱטָאוּ אִמְרוּ בִלְבַבְכֶם עַל־‬ ‫מִשְׁכַּבְכֶם וְדֹמּוּ סֶלָה ׃ ⁶ זִבְחוּ‬ ‫זִבְחֵי־צֶדֶק וּבִטְחוּ אֶל־יְהוָה ׃ ⁷‬ ‫רַבִּים אֹמְרִים מִי־יַרְאֵנוּ טוֹב נְסָה־‬ ‫עָלֵינוּ אוֹר פָּנֶיךָ יְהוָה ׃ ⁸ נָתַתָּה‬ ‫שִׂמְחָה בְלִבִּי מֵעֵת דְּגָנָם וְתִירוֹשָׁם‬ ‫רָבּוּ ׃ ⁹ בְּשָׁלוֹם יַחְדָּו אֶשְׁכְּבָה‬ ‫וְאִישָׁן כִּי־אַתָּה יְהוָה לְבָדָד לָבֶטַח‬ ‫תּוֹשִׁיבֵנִי ׃‬

Targum

Psa. 4:1 For praise, with melodies. A hymn of David. [2] At the time of my prayer, accept [it] from me, O God of my righteousness; at the time of distress, you relieved me; pity me and accept my prayer. [3] O sons of men, why is my glory for humiliation? You will love vanity; you will seek falsehood forever. [4] And they knew, for the LORD has separated the righteous man for himself; the LORD will accept the prayer of David when he calls to him. [5] Tremble for him, and do not sin; utter your petition with your mouth and your request in your heart; and pray upon your beds and remember the days of death forever. [6] Subdue your impulses and it will be reckoned to you as a righteous sacrifice; and hope in the LORD. [7] Many say, "Who will show us good?" Lift on us the light of your countenance, O LORD. [8] You have placed joy in my heart when their grain and their wine has increased. [9] In peace I both lay down and sleep, because you alone are the LORD; in security you will make me dwell.

Superscript

New American Standard 1995	Hebrew
For the choir director; on stringed instruments. A Psalm of David.	לַמְנַצֵּחַ בִּנְגִינוֹת מִזְמוֹר לְדָוִד :

Verse Analysis

David wrote this Psalm while he was fleeing from his first-born Absolom. The Psalm was addressed to David's enemies. David told them to improve their ethics and morality. David declared that Absolom was immoral for revolting against him. A divine decree from the LORD made David King of Israel. Therefore, an attempt to overthrow the King was a sin against the LORD.

Absolom's revolt was due to David's loss of compassion for the LORD's people. The Bathsheba incident caused him to forget that the LORD made him King because of his kindness. David was only caring about himself. The revolt reminded David that he let the Nefesh take over.

לַמְנַצֵּחַ בִּנְגִינוֹת (lam' natzecha ben'geenot) – means "victorious music." This Psalm is a call to the Sefirah Netzach. David believed that the power of music elevates the Ruach to be able to call upon the Sefirot. Netzach can give a person the strength to overcome anything that might disturb his inner peace and serenity.

Verse Rewrite Emphasizing Spiritual Awareness

To the Sefirah Netzach who grants victory through music, a Psalm of David.

Verse One

New American Standard 1995	Hebrew
¹ Answer me when I call, O God of my righteousness! You have relieved me in my distress; Be gracious to me and hear my prayer.	בְּקָרְאִי עֲנֵנִי ׀ אֱלֹהֵי צִדְקִי בַּצָּר הִרְחַבְתָּ לִּי חָנֵּנִי וּשְׁמַע תְּפִלָּתִי׃

Verse Analysis

בְּקָרְאִי עֲנֵנִי (b'kar' ee anaynee) means "proclaim and answer." David offered his prayer and did not demand an immediate answer. David knew that the Shekinah was always close to him and will hear his cry. He let his distress go because he felt the Shekinah with him.

Prayer is victory over distress. Through the power of reasoning, one can discern what is right and true. One must turn to one's knowledge of the LORD as the sole source of the fulfillment of one's desires that one must pledge whatever good the LORD may send so that the LORD's Will would be done in Malkhut.

The vindication David wanted was from the false accusations that Absolom accused him of.

Verse Rewrite Emphasizing Spiritual Awareness

When I pray LORD, I know you will vindicate me because you have taken away my distress in the past.

Verse Two

New American Standard 1995	Hebrew
² O sons of men, how long will my honor become a reproach? *How long* will you love what is worthless and aim at deception? Selah.	בְּנֵי אִישׁ עַד־מֶה כְבוֹדִי לִכְלִמָּה תֶּאֱהָבוּן רִיק תְּבַקְשׁוּ כָזָב סֶלָה׃

Verse Analysis

בְּנֵי אִישׁ (b'nay eesh) means "sons of man." David used this phrase to redirect his remarks from the LORD to humans. David's enemies ridiculed him for calling upon the LORD to help him to defeat his enemies. David's enemies felt prayer itself is a form of self-deception and weakness. These men did not value prayer.

תֶּאֱהָבוּן רִיק (tehehhavon reek) means "empty love." All of a person's ways and deeds are worthless if they do not bring one closer to the LORD.

אִישׁ (ish) – means "man." This word denotes a superior man.

אָדָם (adam) – means "man." This word denotes an ordinary man.

David understood the significance of respecting the monarchy with honor and dignity.

Verse Rewrite Emphasizing Spiritual Awareness

Sons of great men, how long will you respect the monarchy? You love vanity and seek deception. Pause and meditate on this verse.

Verse Three

New American Standard 1995	Hebrew
[3] But know that the LORD has [1a]set apart the [b]godly man for Himself; The LORD [c]hears when I call to Him.	וּדְעוּ כִּי־הִפְלָה יְהוָה חָסִיד לֹו יְהוָה יִשְׁמַע בְּקָרְאִי אֵלָיו:

Verse Analysis

Experience has shown that one should not close one's eyes to what the LORD will do. The Sefirah Chesed will send mercy to all who demonstrate trust in the LORD without reservations.

Verse Rewrite Emphasizing Spiritual Awareness

Know that Chesed will shower people devoted to the LORD its love and mercy, and Chesed will listen when prayer is offered.

Verse Four

New American Standard 1995	Hebrew
⁴ Tremble, and do not sin; Meditate in your heart upon your bed, and be still. Selah.	רִגְזוּ וְאַל־תֶּחֱטָאוּ אִמְרוּ בִלְבַבְכֶם עַל־מִשְׁכַּבְכֶם וְדֹמּוּ סֶלָה

Verse Analysis

רִגְזוּ (reeg'zo) means "be agitated, quiver, quake, be excited, perturbed." This word connotates that he who prays can hope for the Shekinah's nearness throughout one's life. A person can feel the Neshamah, which is a part of the soul.

Homiletically, the verse means that Israel is urged to tremble from the specter of sin to the point where sin becomes disturbing and traumatic. When one goes to sleep, one can think with clarity and objectively because one abandons one's daily pursuits. Forget about the material world and concentrate on the spiritual world.

One should arouse their good inclination to battle evil inclination.

Verse Rewrite Emphasizing Spiritual Awareness

Depart quickly from sinning and sin no more. When you prepare to sleep on your bed, let go of the material world and concentrate on the Spiritual world. Meditate upon this verse.

Verse Five

New American Standard 1995	Hebrew
[5] Offer the sacrifices of righteousness, And trust in the LORD.	זִבְחוּ זִבְחֵי־צֶדֶק וּבִטְחוּ אֶל־יְהוָה׃

Verse Analysis

בְחוּ זִבְחֵי־צֶדֶק (v'who zeev'chay tzedek) means "the slaughter of sacrifice of righteousness." Bring unto the LORD the offering of a dutiful and righteous life. Then place your full trust in the LORD. One must learn how to "tremble" and rejoice" in the LORD's presence. Do not put your trust in the materialistic world but preferably in the spiritual world.

David said to Absalom's followers that they needed to ask for forgiveness, which requires a sacrifice to achieve atonement.

Verse Rewrite Emphasizing Spiritual Awareness

Give to the LORD sacrifices of righteousness and trust the LORD.

Verse Six

New American Standard 1995	Hebrew
[6] Many are saying, "'Who will show us *any* good?" Lift up the light of Your countenance upon us, O LORD!	רַבִּים אֹמְרִים֮ מִי־יַרְאֵ֪נוּ ט֥וֹב נְסָה־עָ֫לֵ֥ינוּ א֤וֹר פָּנֶ֖יךָ יְהוָֽה׃

Verse Analysis

רַבִּים אֹמְרִים (rabeem om' reem) means "many are saying." Many people wish to experience some good. They know that there is only one kind of happiness.

The Shekinah acts in one's life to make one aware of the LORD's presence and keeps us on the right path. The Light of Ein Sof can shine upon all who believe. The Sage Rashi explained that a person should always be content with his/her life if he/she does not look around to find someone living better.

Verse Rewrite Emphasizing Spiritual Awareness

Many people say the Shekinah guides us to mitzvot. May the Light of Ein Sof shine upon us.

Verse Seven

New American Standard 1995	Hebrew
[7] You have put gladness in my heart, More than when their grain and new wine abound.	נָתַ֤תָּה שִׂמְחָ֣ה בְלִבִּ֑י מֵעֵ֬ת דְּגָנָ֖ם וְתִירוֹשָׁ֣ם רָֽבּוּ׃

Verse Analysis

David said to the LORD that he did not have to beg for happiness because he always had received it from the LORD. The LORD implanted in David's heart the trait of being happy with what the LORD has given.

Verse Rewrite Emphasizing Spiritual Awareness

LORD, you put happiness in my heart from the Spiritual World, which is more than from the Material World.

Verse Eight

New American Standard 1995	Hebrew
[8] In peace I will both lie down and sleep, For You alone, O LORD, make me to dwell in safety.	בְּשָׁל֣וֹם יַחְדָּו֮ אֶשְׁכְּבָ֪ה וְאִ֫ישָׁ֥ן כִּֽי־אַתָּ֣ה יְהוָ֣ה לְבָדָ֑ד לָבֶ֖טַח תּוֹשִׁיבֵֽנִי׃

Verse Analysis

Even though David's enemies surrounded him, his trust was in the LORD, who protected him. David slept comfortably because the Shekinah was with him. The Shekinah felt like a wall surrounding him, so he knew no one could harm him.

The verse can be seen as an appeal for peace and unity.

Verse Rewrite Emphasizing Spiritual Awareness

LORD, give me unity and a place of safety and peace.

Complete Psalm Rewrite Emphasizing Spiritual Awareness

To the Sefirah Netzach who grants victory through music, a Psalm of David. When I pray LORD, I know you will vindicate me because you have taken away my distress in the past.

Sons of great men, how long will you respect the monarchy? You love vanity and seek deception. Pause and meditate on this verse.

Know that Chesed will shower people devoted to the LORD its love and mercy, and Chesed will listen when prayer is offered.

Depart quickly from sinning and sin no more. When you prepare to sleep on your bed, let go of the material world and concentrate on the Spiritual world. Meditate upon this verse.

Give to the LORD sacrifices of righteousness and trust the LORD.

Many people say the Shekinah guides us to mitzvot. May the Light of Ein Sof shine upon us.

LORD, you put happiness in my heart from the Spiritual World, which is more than from the Material World.

LORD, give me unity and a place of safety and peace.

Language

New American Standard 1995	Hebrew
0 For the choir director; for flute accompaniment. A Psalm of David. 1 Give ear to my words, O LORD, Consider my groaning. 2 Heed the sound of my cry for help, my King and my God, For to You I pray. 3 In the morning, O LORD, You will hear my voice; In the morning I will order *my prayer* to You and *eagerly* watch. 4 For You are not a God who takes pleasure in wickedness; No evil dwells with You. 5 The boastful shall not stand before Your eyes; You hate all who do iniquity. 6 You destroy those who speak falsehood; The LORD abhors the man of bloodshed and deceit. 7 But as for me, by Your abundant lovingkindness I will enter Your house, At Your holy temple I will bow in reverence for You. 8 O LORD, lead me in Your righteousness because of my foes; Make Your way straight before me. 9 There is nothing reliable in what they say; Their inward part is destruction *itself.* Their throat is an open grave; They flatter with their tongue. 10 Hold them guilty, O God; By their own devices let them fall! In the multitude of their transgressions thrust them out, For they are rebellious against You.	לַמְנַצֵּחַ אֶל־הַנְּחִילוֹת מִזְמוֹר Psa. 5:1 לְדָוִד : 2 אֲמָרַי הַאֲזִינָה וְיהוָה בִּינָה הֲגִיגִי : 3 הַקְשִׁיבָה וְלְקוֹל שַׁוְעִי מַלְכִּי וֵאלֹהָי כִּי־אֵלֶיךָ אֶתְפַּלָּל : 4 יְהוָה בֹּקֶר תִּשְׁמַע קוֹלִי בֹּקֶר אֶעֱרָךְ־לְךָ וַאֲצַפֶּה : 5 כִּי לֹא אֵל־חָפֵץ רֶשַׁע אָתָּה לֹא יְגֻרְךָ רָע : 6 לֹא־יִתְיַצְּבוּ הוֹלְלִים לְנֶגֶד עֵינֶיךָ שָׂנֵאתָ כָּל־פֹּעֲלֵי אָוֶן : 7 תְּאַבֵּד דֹּבְרֵי כָזָב אִישׁ־דָּמִים וּמִרְמָה יְתָעֵב וְיהוָה : 8 וַאֲנִי בְּרֹב חַסְדְּךָ אָבוֹא בֵיתֶךָ אֶשְׁתַּחֲוֶה אֶל־הֵיכַל־קָדְשְׁךָ בְּיִרְאָתֶךָ : 9 יְהוָה נְחֵנִי בְצִדְקָתֶךָ לְמַעַן שׁוֹרְרָי הוֹשַׁר [הַיְשַׁר] לְפָנַי דַּרְכֶּךָ : 10 כִּי אֵין בְּפִיהוּ נְכוֹנָה קִרְבָּם הַוּוֹת קֶבֶר־פָּתוּחַ גְּרוֹנָם לְשׁוֹנָם יַחֲלִיקוּן : 11 הַאֲשִׁימֵם אֱלֹהִים יִפְּלוּ מִמֹּעֲצוֹתֵיהֶם בְּרֹב פִּשְׁעֵיהֶם הַדִּיחֵמוֹ כִּי־מָרוּ בָךְ : 12 וְיִשְׂמְחוּ כָל־חוֹסֵי בָךְ לְעוֹלָם יְרַנֵּנוּ וְתָסֵךְ עָלֵימוֹ וְיַעְלְצוּ בְךָ אֹהֲבֵי שְׁמֶךָ : 13 כִּי־אַתָּה תְּבָרֵךְ צַדִּיק יְהוָה כַּצִּנָּה רָצוֹן תַּעְטְרֶנּוּ :

¹¹ But let all who take refuge in You be glad, Let them ever sing for joy; And may You shelter them, That those who love Your name may exult in You.
¹² For it is You who blesses the righteous man, O LORD, You surround him with favor as with a shield.

Targum

Psa. 5:1 For praise, with dancing. A hymn of David. ² Hear my utterance, O LORD, consider my murmuring. ³ Hear the sound of my petition, my king and God, for I will pray in your presence. ⁴ O LORD, in the morning hear my voice; in the morning I set myself before you and keep watch. ⁵ Because you are not a God who takes pleasure in wickedness; evil did not abide with you. ⁶ Scoffers shall not stand before your eyes; you hate all deeds of falsehood. ⁷ You will destroy tellers of lies; the LORD will loath the man who sheds innocent blood and the deceiver. ⁸ And I, through your great goodness, will enter your house; I will bow down to your temple in awe of you. ⁹ O LORD, guide me by your righteousness; because of my hymn, make firm your paths before me. ¹⁰ Because there is no reliability in the mouths of the wicked; their bodies are full of tumult; like Sheol, their throat is open; their tongues flatter. ¹¹ God has accused them; they will be done away with by their counsel; for their great sin he overturned them, for they rebelled against your command. ¹² And all who trust in your word will rejoice forever; they will give praise and you will protect them; and those who love your name will rejoice in you. ¹³ Because you will bless the righteous, O LORD; as with a shield, you will crown him with good will.

Superscript

New American Standard 1995	Hebrew
[0] For the choir director; for flute accompaniment. A Psalm of David.	לַמְנַצֵּחַ אֶל־הַנְּחִילוֹת מִזְמוֹר לְדָוִד׃

Verse Analysis

This Psalm describes the causes of the revolt that Absalom and his friends held against King David. The main target of the Psalm is Achitophel, whose crimes surpassed that of the people. Achtophel took the most authentic Jewish concepts, the Holy Torah itself, and grotesquely distorted it to serve his own ambitions. He was only interested in material gains in the material world. He yearned for power, honor, and riches.

Achitophel did not view the Torah as an inheritance from the LORD. He was not proud to receive the Torah from his teachers, so his Torah was not genuine.

The Psalm was dedicated to condemning the insincere.

אֶל־הַנְּחִילוֹת (el – han'cheelot) – denotes an inheritance and also the maintenance of spiritual values that are to be preserved forever. It also denotes the final achievements attained by humans on Earth through loyalty – or disloyalty to the LORD. The LORD assigns righteousness to good people. The LORD does not assign anything to wicked people.

The Sage Radak said that הַנְּחִילוֹת literally means "a swarm of bees" because this word is the name of a musical instrument because it makes a droning bee sound.

The Psalm was dedicated when King David was under attack. The droning buzzing sound captured the mood of the enemy hordes who swarmed around Israel like angry buzzing bees.

Verse Rewrite Emphasizing Spiritual Awareness

The sound of the Nechilos tells us about achieving life's goals, a Psalm of David.

Verse One and Two

New American Standard 1995	Hebrew
¹ Give ear to my words, O LORD, Consider my groaning. ² Heed the sound of my cry for help, my King and my God, For to You I pray.	אֲמָרַי הַאֲזִינָה ׀ יְהֹוָה בִּינָה ²: הֲגִיגִי ³ הַקְשִׁיבָה ׀ לְקוֹל שַׁוְעִי מַלְכִּי וֵאלֹהָי כִּי־אֵלֶיךָ אֶתְפַּלָּל׃

Verse Analysis

אֲמָרַי (amara) – means "words." This word denotes those thoughts that have already become clear enough to be expressed in words. The Sage Rashi said that this means that when David could express his wants to the LORD that he hoped the LORD would listen and respond.

הַאֲזִינָה (haazeenah) – means "to give." It denotes to incline the ear for the reception of hearing one's thoughts. The Sage Rashi said that when David was fearful or worried, he had a difficult time praying to the LORD. When that occurred, David hoped that the LORD would hear his needs and help him.

David beseeched the LORD's nearness for all the impulses from his soul. He desired the LORD's presence in his speech, his thinking, and his prayers.

הַקְשִׁיבָה (hak' wheevah) – means "to heed." This word denotes a more intensive form of listening.

Verse Rewrite Emphasizing Spiritual Awareness

1 Hear my wants, oh LORD, mainly when I cannot express them myself.

2 Listen deeply to my words my LORD, for I pray to you my deepest thoughts.

Verse Three

New American Standard 1995	Hebrew
³ In the morning, O LORD, You will hear my voice; In the morning I will order *my prayer* to You and *eagerly* watch.	יְהוָה בֹּקֶר תִּשְׁמַע קוֹלִי בֹּקֶר אֶעֱרָךְ־לְךָ וַאֲצַפֶּה׃

Verse Analysis

בֹּקֶר (bokar) – means "morning, dawn." Linked with the root בָּקָר, בֹּקֶר denotes the breaking through of the daylight and thus dawn or, more usually, morning. This noun is peculiar to Hebrew though the assumed root is not. In the first part of the verse, this word intends to denote a time of day. The second time the word occurs, it is meant to indicate the dawning of a new day in the history of humankind.

A period of disaster is always referred to as "night," the dawning of salvation is described in the allegorical simile of "morning" or "dawn."

The LORD's justice (Gevurah) will hand out the final and fitting fate to the righteous and the wicked, each according to his/her merits. This plainly shows to the world the distinction between the righteous and the wicked.

David talked about a time when righteousness and fear of the LORD will reign supreme on the Earth. It will be a bright dawn and cloudless morning. David liked to pray in the early morning. Praying in the morning is good because the requirements of the day have not consumed all of one's time. David said that he did not precede his prayers with his own personal pursuits.

וָאֲצַפֶּה (vaatzageh) – means "to watch." The Sage Rashi said that this denotes that David anticipated the punishment for the wicked.

Verse Rewrite Emphasizing Spiritual Awareness

LORD in the morning, I pray you can hear my voice as I prepare myself for you, and I anticipate your justice on the righteous and wicked.

New American Standard 1995	Hebrew
[4] For You are not a God who takes pleasure in wickedness; No evil dwells with You. [5] The boastful shall not stand before Your eyes; You hate all who do iniquity. [6] You destroy those who speak falsehood; The LORD abhors the man of bloodshed and deceit.	כִּי ׀ לֹא אֵל־חָפֵץ רֶשַׁע ׀ אַתָּה 5 לֹא יְגֻרְךָ רָע׃ 6 לֹא־יִתְיַצְּבוּ ־הוֹלְלִים לְנֶגֶד עֵינֶיךָ שָׂנֵאתָ כָּל תְּאַבֵּד דֹּבְרֵי כָזָב 7 פֹּעֲלֵי אָוֶן׃ אִישׁ־דָּמִים וּמִרְמָה יְתָעֵב ׀ יְהוָה׃

Verse Analysis

The gloom of the night has covered the history of humanity and society. In a lawless society, evil prevails. Men and women who do violence, who misuse their power, seem to reap tribute and goodwill everywhere. Some people seek to attain their goals, not by means of truth and uprighteousness but by deceit. The LORD will not allow a wicked person to have a permanent place in this world nor the world to come.

The LORD is a God of righteousness and truth. Deceit is as hateful to the LORD, as is murder. Where there is Godliness, there can be no evil.

Verse Rewrite Emphasizing Spiritual Awareness

⁴ You are not a God who takes pleasure in wickedness; wherever your Godliness is, evil cannot exist.

⁵ The boastful shall not stand before Your eyes; You hate all who are deceitful.

⁶ You destroy those who speak falsehood; The LORD abhors the man of bloodshed and deceit.

Verse Seven

New American Standard 1995	Hebrew
[7] But as for me, by Your abundant lovingkindness I will enter Your house, At Your holy temple I will bow in reverence for You.	וַאֲנִי בְּרֹב חַסְדְּךָ אָבוֹא בֵיתֶךָ אֶשְׁתַּחֲוֶה אֶל־הֵיכַל־קָדְשְׁךָ בְּיִרְאָתֶךָ :

Verse Analysis

There is no future for evil or wicked people. David had to suffer at the hands of deceitful men, particularly by the hands of Achitophel. Achitophel was well skilled in the art of deceit. David being Jewish, was privileged to partake in all gifts from the LORD.

The sanctuary allowed the LORD to teach people how to fashion their lives on Earth so that His Presence will dwell among them even in dark days. David entered the LORD's Temple to thank the LORD for the kindness the LORD heaped upon him by showing David that revenge had been taken upon his enemies.

When David says "your house" and "Holy Sanctuary" he meant the Holy of Holies, the resting place of the Holy Ark.

Verse Rewrite Emphasizing Spiritual Awareness

Nevertheless, as for me, because of your abundant kindness, LORD, I want to enter your Holy Sanctuary.

Verse Eight

New American Standard 1995	Hebrew
8 O LORD, lead me in Your righteousness because of my foes; Make Your way straight before me.	יְהוָה ׀ וְנְחֵנִי בְצִדְקָתֶךָ לְמַעַן 9 שׁוֹרְרָי הוֹשַׁר [הַיְשַׁר] לְפָנַי דַּרְכֶּךָ ׃

Verse Analysis

נְחֵנִי (n'chainee) – means "to lead or guide." David asked for help from the LORD that he would be able to recognize the right path and not miss it. David needed the LORD to place the right path before him. David always relied on the LORD; thus, it was not David's decision to determine the right path. The LORD determined David's correct path in life.

A person must do a significant part of the work in the effort of discerning what is right. David's enemies watched him in the hope that he would betray the LORD – then the LORD might desert him.

Verse Rewrite Emphasizing Spiritual Awareness

LORD help me so I may recognize the right path because my enemies watch over me looking for my failures, place the right path before me.

Verse Nine

New American Standard 1995	Hebrew
9 There is nothing reliable in what they say; Their inward part is destruction *itself*. Their throat is an open grave; They flatter with their tongue.	כִּי אֵין בְּפִיהוּ נְכוֹנָה֮ קִרְבָּם֮ 10׃ קֶבֶר־פָּתוּחַ גְּרוֹנָם לְשׁוֹנָם יַחֲלִיקוּן׃

Verse Analysis

יַחֲלִיקוּן (yachaleekon) – means "to flatter." David was referring to the scheming minds of his enemies. Their throats were an open portal for Sheol. They coated their tongues with such smooth words that anyone who put their trust in them was hopelessly doomed to fall into the grave dug by those plotters of evil.

David was careful because his enemies were always watching him. They were waiting for any errors by David to attack him.

קֶבֶר־פָּתוּחַ גְּרוֹנָם (kaevaer gatoocha g' ronam) – means "open grave throat." The Sage Rashi said David's enemies sought to swallow the fruits of other people's labors, just as an open grave takes in the corpse

Verse Rewrite Emphasizing Spiritual Awareness

Their spirit is looking for ways to destroy me, they seek to swallow the fruits of other people like the open grave takes in the corpse.

Verse Ten

New American Standard 1995	Hebrew
[10] Hold them guilty, O God; By their own devices let them fall! In the multitude of their transgressions thrust them out, For they are rebellious against You.	הַאֲשִׁימֵ֨ם ׀ אֱלֹהִ֗ים יִפְּלוּ֮ ¹¹ מִֽמֹּעֲצ֫וֹתֵיהֶ֥ם בְּרֹ֣ב פִּ֭שְׁעֵיהֶם הַדִּיחֵ֑מוֹ כִּי־מָ֥רוּ בָֽךְ׃

Verse Analysis

הַאֲשִׁימֵ֨ם (haasheemaym) – means "guilty." This word denotes the destruction which the sinner has brought upon himself. It usually refers to that downfall, which comes as a result of crimes committed against society.

David wanted his enemies sent away because of the multitude of their crimes, and they should lose all the prosperity which they possessed or might yet amass.

David asked the LORD to bring his enemies to justice (Gevurah) and convict them of their guilt and cast them down from their positions of eminence.

Verse Rewrite Emphasizing Spiritual Awareness

May Gevurah act upon them because of their ways, for their many sins Gevurah must cast them away.

Verse Eleven

New American Standard 1995	Hebrew
11 But let all who take refuge in You be glad, Let them ever sing for joy; And may You shelter them, That those who love Your name may exult in You.	וְיִשְׂמְחוּ כָל־חוֹסֵי בָךְ לְעוֹלָם יְרַנֵּנוּ וְתָסֵךְ עָלֵימוֹ וְיַעְלְצוּ בְךָ אֹהֲבֵי שְׁמֶךָ׃

Verse Analysis

וְיִשְׂמְחוּ (v'yees' m'chu) means "to rejoice." David said that the fall of his adversaries and their destruction was brought upon by themselves. It was through their criminal scheming their destruction came. Justice (Gevurah) dealt with them.

David said that by destroying his enemies, the LORD gave shelter to all those who are threatened by foes.

In David's era, darkness was occurring because of human sins. An unshakable trust in the LORD's name reveals His ways and purpose. That trust upholds persons who are faithful to their deity and the LORD's law and can keep them sure of the dawn in humankind's history that must come one day.

The Sage Rashi said "You topple the wicked all who trust in you will be glad."

Joy should be in the LORD and not material things.

וְיַעְלְצוּ (v'ya'l'tzoo) means "to exult or rejoice." This word is used to describe spiritual not physical joy.

Verse Rewrite Emphasizing Spiritual Awareness

All who put their trust in You will rejoice with good cheer and LORD You give shelter to all persons who love your Name and shall experience spiritual joy.

Verse Twelve

New American Standard 1995	Hebrew
[12] For it is You who blesses the righteous man, O LORD, You surround him with favor as with a shield.	כִּי־אַתָּה תְּבָרֵךְ צַדִּיק יְהוָה כַּצִּנָּה רָצוֹן תַּעְטְרֶנּוּ׃

Verse Analysis

Lawless men vainly seek to attain prosperity simply by human shrewdness and force. Righteous men receive blessings from the hands of the LORD. Lawlessness seeks evil – you can only temporarily squelch evil because it will always return.

By elevating the spirit of humans, the LORD helps humans attain a proper discernment between the different methods used in the pursuit of the ultimate goal of humanity and thus makes humans victorious over evil.

Verse Rewrite Emphasizing Spiritual Awareness

LORD, I know you will bless the righteous surrounding them like a shield.

Complete Psalm Rewrite Emphasizing Spiritual Awareness

0 The sound of the Nechilos tells us about achieving life's goals, a Psalm of David.

1 Hear my wants, oh LORD, mainly when I cannot express them myself.

2 Listen deeply to my words my LORD, for I pray to you my deepest thoughts.

3 LORD in the morning, I pray you can hear my voice as I prepare myself for you, and I anticipate your justice on the righteous and wicked.

4 You are not a God who takes pleasure in wickedness; wherever your Godliness is, evil cannot exist.

5 The boastful shall not stand before Your eyes; You hate all who are deceitful.

6 You destroy those who speak falsehood; The LORD abhors the man of bloodshed and deceit.

7 Nevertheless, as for me, because of your abundant kindness, LORD, I want to enter your Holy Sanctuary.

LORD help me so I may recognize the right path because my enemies watch over me looking for my failures, place the right path before me.

9 Their spirit is looking for ways to destroy me, they seek to swallow the fruits of other people like the open grave takes in the corpse.

10 May Gevurah act upon them because of their ways, for their many sins Gevurah must cast them away.

11 All who put their trust in You will rejoice with good cheer and LORD You give shelter to all persons who love your Name and shall experience spiritual joy.

12 LORD, I know you will bless the righteous surrounding them like a shield

Language

New American Standard 1995	Hebrew
0 For the choir director; with stringed instruments, upon an eight-string lyre. A Psalm of David. **1** O LORD, do not rebuke me in Your anger, Nor chasten me in Your wrath. **2** Be gracious to me, O LORD, for I *am* pining away; Heal me, O LORD, for my bones are dismayed. **3** And my soul is greatly dismayed; But You, O LORD — how long? **4** Return, O LORD, rescue my soul; save me because of Your lovingkindness. **5** For there is no mention of You in death; In Sheol who will give You thanks? **6** I am weary with my sighing; Every night I make my bed swim, I dissolve my couch with my tears. **7** My eye has wasted away with grief; It has become old because of all my adversaries. **8** Depart from me, all you who do iniquity, For the LORD has heard the voice of my weeping. **9** The LORD has heard my supplication, the LORD receives my prayer. **10** All my enemies will be ashamed and greatly dismayed; they shall turn back, they will suddenly be ashamed.	לַמְנַצֵּחַ בִּנְגִינוֹת עַל־הַשְּׁמִינִית מִזְמוֹר לְדָוִד׃ 2 יְהוָה אַל־בְּאַפְּךָ תוֹכִיחֵנִי וְאַל־בַּחֲמָתְךָ תְיַסְּרֵנִי׃ 3 חָנֵּנִי יְהוָה כִּי אֻמְלַל אָנִי רְפָאֵנִי יְהוָה כִּי נִבְהֲלוּ עֲצָמָי׃ 4 וְנַפְשִׁי נִבְהֲלָה מְאֹד וְאַתְּ [וְ][אַתָּה] יְהוָה עַד־מָתָי׃ 5 שׁוּבָה יְהוָה חַלְּצָה נַפְשִׁי הוֹשִׁיעֵנִי לְמַעַן חַסְדֶּךָ׃ 6 כִּי אֵין בַּמָּוֶת זִכְרֶךָ בִּשְׁאוֹל מִי יוֹדֶה־ לָּךְ׃ 7 יָגַעְתִּי בְּאַנְחָתִי אַשְׂחֶה בְכָל־לַיְלָה מִטָּתִי בְּדִמְעָתִי עַרְשִׂי אַמְסֶה׃ 8 עָשְׁשָׁה מִכַּעַס עֵינִי עָתְקָה בְּכָל־צוֹרְרָי׃ 9 סוּרוּ מִמֶּנִּי כָּל־פֹּעֲלֵי אָוֶן כִּי־שָׁמַע יְהוָה קוֹל בִּכְיִי׃ 10 שָׁמַע יְהוָה תְּחִנָּתִי יְהוָה תְּפִלָּתִי יִקָּח׃ 11 יֵבֹשׁוּ וְיִבָּהֲלוּ מְאֹד כָּל־אֹיְבָי יָשֻׁבוּ יֵבֹשׁוּ רָגַע׃

Psalm Targum

[1] For praise; with melodies on the harp of eight strings. A hymn of David. [2] O LORD, do not humble me in your anger; and do not punish me in your wrath. [3] Pity me, O LORD, for I am weak; heal me, O LORD, for my bones are terrified. [4] And my soul is greatly terrified; and you, O LORD, when will you give me relief? [5] Turn, O LORD, save my soul, redeem me for the sake of your goodness. [6] For there is no memory of you in death; in Sheol who will give you thanks? [7] I am wearied with my groaning; I will speak in my sorrow every night on my bed; I will drown my couch with my tears. [8] My eye is dark from my trouble; it is worn out by all my oppressors. [9] Leave me, all doers of falsehood; for the LORD has heard the sound of my weeping. [10] My petition has been heard in the LORD's presence; the LORD will accept my prayer. [11] All of my enemies will be ashamed and very afraid; they will turn and be ashamed in an instant.

Superscript

New American Standard 1995	Hebrew
[0] For the choir director; with stringed instruments, upon an eight-string lyre. A Psalm of David.	לַמְנַצֵּחַ בִּנְגִינוֹת עַל־הַשְּׁמִינִית מִזְמוֹר לְדָוִד׃

Verse Analysis

The psalmist wants to raise the human spirit from a state of utter despair. It is futile at times to expect help from men. The psalmist has confidence in the LORD that He will intervene with His saving power at the time when it is most needed.

Harps

- seven-string harp is symbolic of the LORD's creation
- eight-string harp is symbolic of the Messianic age

Hymns played in the Temple, which praised the LORD's presence on Earth, were played on the seven-string harp. The hymns of the Messiah will be played on the eight-string harp. At that time, the final redemption (Tikkun) will come.

Verse Rewrite Emphasizing Spiritual Awareness

To Him who offers victory through the playing of the Sheminis (8 string harp), a song of David.

Verse One

New American Standard 1995	Hebrew
[1] O LORD, do not rebuke me in Your anger, Nor chasten me in Your wrath.	יְהוָה אַל־בְּאַפְּךָ תוֹכִיחֵנִי וְאַל־בַּחֲמָתְךָ [2] תְיַסְּרֵנִי׃

Verse Analysis

The LORD gave a sign to express His anger to help David realize his error. David accepted divine punishment because he deserved it. David asked the LORD to not send His rebuke to him.

Verse Rewrite Emphasizing Spiritual Awareness

LORD, I know I deserve your punishment from Gevurah, please do not allow it to be sent.

Verse Two

New American Standard 1995	Hebrew
² Be gracious to me, O LORD, for I *am* pining away; Heal me, O LORD, for my bones are dismayed.	³ חָנֵּנִי יְהוָה כִּי אֻמְלַל אָנִי רְפָאֵנִי יְהוָה כִּי נִבְהֲלוּ עֲצָמָי :

Verse Analysis

The LORD may have given David renewed vigor, not because he was deserving of grace but because he was already completely broken and devoid of strength. David felt his bones would support him as a seat of strength but was stricken and made him completely powerless. David prayed for mercy (Chesed), to stop judgment (Gevurah) from agitating him. David also asked the LORD to hold back any future punishment.

David's most significant pain was not physical but rather mental anguish – the thought of sinning.

Verse Rewrite Emphasizing Spiritual Awareness

LORD, I am broken and feeble. Heal me because I am broken down to the bones.

Verse Three

New American Standard 1995	Hebrew
³ And my soul is greatly dismayed; But You, O LORD — how long?	וְנַפְשִׁי נִבְהֲלָה מְאֹד וְאַתְּ [וְ][אַתָּה] יְהוָֹה ⁴ עַד־מָתָי:

Verse Analysis

David's soul was in utter despair. He had lost all hope for his body and his spirit. David knew that the LORD could restore the soul. There are people who realize that physical alignment can be a gift from the LORD, which can cleanse and mend the soiled and tattered soil.

Verse Rewrite Emphasizing Spiritual Awareness

My Nefesh (body) and Ruach (spirit) utterly despair, but you LORD can help me, when?

Verse Four

New American Standard 1995	Hebrew
[4] Return, O LORD, rescue my soul; save me because of Your lovingkindness.	שׁוּבָה יְהוָה חַלְּצָה נַפְשִׁי הוֹשִׁיעֵנִי לְמַעַן חַסְדֶּךָ׃

Verse Analysis

David thought that the LORD turned away from him because of his sins. He asked the LORD to free his soul from the spiritual forces that paralyzed him. All infirmities of the body stem from blemishes and sins of the soul. David requested that the LORD release his soul by forgiving him.

Verse Rewrite Emphasizing Spiritual Awareness

LORD release my Nefesh and Ruach from agony through your kindness.

Verse Five

New American Standard 1995	Hebrew
[5] For there is no mention of You in death; In Sheol who will give You thanks?	כִּי אֵין בַּמָּוֶת זִכְרֶךָ בִּשְׁאוֹל מִי יוֹדֶה־לָּךְ: [6]

Verse Analysis

Death is a consequence of the law of nature handed down by the LORD when the world began and thus is merely a manifestation of the existence of the order of nature, the power of which no one can escape.

To the heathen mind, the power of its idols is demonstrated when these deities overthrow the strongest of human forces, a display of the degraded lethal force to which all living things succumb. This is so because the heathen deities are, in reality, the force of nature ordained by the LORD.

David told the LORD that he could not praise or mention His name if he is dead.

Verse Rewrite Emphasizing Spiritual Awareness

In death, there is no way to praise you, LORD, so who will praise you?

Verse Six, Seven, Eight

New American Standard 1995	Hebrew
[6] I am weary with my sighing; Every night I make my bed swim, I dissolve my couch with my tears. [7] My eye has wasted away with grief; It has become old because of all my adversaries. [8] Depart from me, all you who do iniquity, For the LORD has heard the voice of my weeping.	יָגַ֤עְתִּי ׀ בְּֽאַנְחָתִ֗י אַשְׂחֶ֣ה בְכָל־ לַ֭יְלָה מִטָּתִ֑י בְּ֝דִמְעָתִ֗י עַרְשִׂ֥י אַמְסֶֽה׃ עָשְׁשָׁ֣ה מִכַּ֣עַס עֵינִ֑י עָ֝תְקָ֗ה בְּכָל־ צוֹרְרָֽי׃ [9] סוּרוּ מִ֭מֶּנִּי כָּל־פֹּ֣עֲלֵי אָ֑וֶן כִּֽי־שָׁמַ֥ע יְ֝הוָ֗ה ק֣וֹל בִּכְיִֽי׃

Verse Analysis

David could not see well because of his grief due to his sin. David cried so much while in bed it became foul-smelling.

Verse Rewrite Emphasizing Spiritual Awareness

V6 – I am worried with sadness. Every night I cry so much that my bed is soaked with tears.

V7 – I am so upset that I cannot see because of these people who oppress me.

V8 – Leave me all sinners, for the LORD heard the sound of my crying.

Verse Nine

New American Standard 1995	Hebrew
[9] The LORD has heard my supplication, the LORD receives my prayer.	[10] שָׁמַע יְהוָה תְּחִנָּתִי יְהוָה תְּפִלָּתִי יִקָּח׃

.

Verse Rewrite Emphasizing Spiritual Awareness

The LORD heard my plea and will accept my prayer.

Verse Ten

New American Standard 1995	Hebrew
10 All my enemies will be ashamed and greatly dismayed; they shall turn back, they will suddenly be ashamed.	יֵבֹ֤שׁוּ ׀ וְיִבָּהֲל֣וּ מְאֹד֮ כָּל־אֹיְבָ֥י ‏11 יָשֻׁ֥בוּ יֵבֹ֖שׁוּ רָֽגַע׃

Verse Rewrite Emphasizing Spiritual Awareness

All my foes will be deceived and terrified; they will regret and be instantly shamed.

Complete Psalm Rewrite Emphasizing Spiritual Awareness

To Him who offers victory through the playing of the Sheminis (8 string harp), a song of David.

LORD, I know I deserve your punishment from Gevurah, please do not allow it to be sent.

LORD, I am broken and feeble. Heal me because I am broken down to the bones.

My Nefesh (body) and Ruach (spirit) utterly despair, but you LORD can help me, when?

LORD release my Nefesh and Ruach from agony through your kindness.

In death, there is no way to praise you, LORD, so who will praise you?

I am worried with sadness. Every night I cry so much that my bed is soaked with tears.

I am so upset that I cannot see because of these people who oppress me.

Leave me all sinners, for the LORD heard the sound of my crying.

The LORD heard my plea and will accept my prayer.

All my foes will be deceived and terrified; they will regret and be instantly shamed.

Language

New American Standard 1995	Hebrew
Psa. 7:0 A Shiggaion of David, which he sang to the LORD concerning Cush, a Benjamite. Psa. 7:1 O LORD my God, in You I have taken refuge; Save me from all those who pursue me, and deliver me, ² Or he will tear my soul like a lion, Dragging me away, while there is none to deliver. Psa. 7:3 O LORD my God, if I have done this, If there is injustice in my hands, ⁴ If I have rewarded evil to my friend, Or have plundered him who without cause was my adversary, ⁵ Let the enemy pursue my soul and overtake *it*; And let him trample my life down to the ground And lay my glory in the dust. Selah. Psa. 7:6 Arise, O LORD, in Your anger; Lift up Yourself against the rage of my adversaries, And arouse Yourself for me; You have appointed judgment. ⁷ Let the assembly of the peoples encompass You, And over them return on high. ⁸ The LORD judges the peoples; Vindicate me, O LORD, according to my righteousness and my integrity that is in me. ⁹ O let the evil of the wicked come to an end, but establish the righteous; For the righteous God tries the hearts and minds. ¹⁰ My shield is with God, Who saves the upright in heart. ¹¹ God is a righteous judge, And a God who has indignation every day.	שִׁגָּיוֹן לְדָוִד אֲשֶׁר־שָׁר לַיהוָה עַל־דִּבְרֵי־כוּשׁ בֶּן־יְמִינִי׃ 2 יְהוָה אֱלֹהַי בְּךָ חָסִיתִי הוֹשִׁיעֵנִי מִכָּל־רֹדְפַי וְהַצִּילֵנִי׃ 3 פֶּן־ יִטְרֹף כְּאַרְיֵה נַפְשִׁי פֹּרֵק וְאֵין מַצִּיל׃ 4 יְהוָה אֱלֹהַי אִם־ עָשִׂיתִי זֹאת אִם־יֶשׁ־עָוֶל בְּכַפָּי׃ 5 אִם־גָּמַלְתִּי שׁוֹלְמִי רָע וָאֲחַלְּצָה צוֹרְרִי רֵיקָם׃ 6 יִרַדֹּף אוֹיֵב וְנַפְשִׁי וְיַשֵּׂג וְיִרְמֹס לָאָרֶץ חַיָּי וּכְבוֹדִי וְלֶעָפָר יַשְׁכֵּן סֶלָה׃ 7 קוּמָה יְהוָה בְּאַפֶּךָ הִנָּשֵׂא בְּעַבְרוֹת צוֹרְרָי וְעוּרָה אֵלַי מִשְׁפָּט צִוִּיתָ׃ 8 וַעֲדַת לְאֻמִּים תְּסוֹבְבֶךָּ וְעָלֶיהָ לַמָּרוֹם שׁוּבָה׃ 9 יְהוָה יָדִין עַמִּים שָׁפְטֵנִי יְהוָה כְּצִדְקִי וּכְתֻמִּי עָלָי׃ 10 יִגְמָר־נָא רַע וּרְשָׁעִים וּתְכוֹנֵן צַדִּיק וּבֹחֵן לִבּוֹת וּכְלָיוֹת אֱלֹהִים צַדִּיק׃ 11 מָגִנִּי

Psa. 7:12 If a man does not repent, He will sharpen His sword; He has bent His bow and made it ready.

13 He has also prepared 'for Himself deadly weapons; He makes His arrows fiery shafts.

14 Behold, he travails with wickedness, And he conceives mischief and brings forth falsehood.

15 He has dug a pit and hollowed it out, And has fallen into the hole which he made.

16 His mischief will return upon his own head, And his violence will descend upon his own pate.

Psa. 7:17 I will give thanks to the LORD according to His righteousness And will sing praise to the name of the LORD Most High.

עַל־אֱלֹהִים מוֹשִׁיעַ יִשְׁרֵי־לֵב:

12 אֱלֹהִים שׁוֹפֵט צַדִּיק וְאֵל זֹעֵם בְּכָל־יוֹם: 13 אִם־לֹא יָשׁוּב חַרְבּוֹ יִלְטוֹשׁ קַשְׁתּוֹ דָרַךְ וַיְכוֹנְנֶהָ: 14 וְלוֹ הֵכִין כְּלֵי־מָוֶת חִצָּיו לְדֹלְקִים יִפְעָל: 15 הִנֵּה יְחַבֶּל־אָוֶן וְהָרָה עָמָל וְיָלַד שָׁקֶר: 16 בּוֹר כָּרָה וַיַּחְפְּרֵהוּ וַיִּפֹּל בְּשַׁחַת יִפְעָל: 17 יָשׁוּב עֲמָלוֹ בְרֹאשׁוֹ וְעַל קָדְקָדוֹ חֲמָסוֹ יֵרֵד: 18 אוֹדֶה יְהוָה כְּצִדְקוֹ וַאֲזַמְּרָה שֵׁם־יְהוָה עֶלְיוֹן:

Psa. 7:1 A rendition of the thanksgiving of David, who gave praise to the LORD; for he spoke a song about the ruin of Saul son of Kish, from the tribe of Benjamin. [2] O LORD my God, I have trusted in your word; deliver me from all my persecutors and save me. [3] Lest he crush my soul like a lion; he will tear and there is no one who will deliver me. [4] O LORD my God, if I have made this song with evil intent, if there is oppression in my hand, [5] If I have repaid my ally with evil, or thrust away my oppressor for nothing, [6] May the enemy pursue my soul, and may he overtake and trample my life to the ground, and may my honor rest in the dust forever. [7] Arise, O LORD, in your might; be lifted up in anger against my oppressors; and bring hastily to me the justice that you commanded. [8] The gathering of the nations will surround you; because of it return to the place of your presence. [9] The word of the LORD will judge the Gentiles; judge me, O LORD, by my merit, and for my innocence recompense me. [10] Now may the evil of the wicked perish; and let the righteous be firmly established; and the righteous God examines hearts and minds. [11] My shield is on God, redeemer of the upright of heart. [12] God is the righteous judge, and in might is angry at the wicked every day. [13] If one does not repent and reverence him, his sword is whetted, his bow drawn and ready. [14] On his account, he has prepared the weapons of death; he will make his arrows for those who pursue the righteous. [15] Behold, he will be in pains with falsehood, and will conceive trouble, and give birth to falsehood. [16] He has dug a pit and deepened it; and he fell in the pit he made. [17] His misery will return on his head; and on his pate his rapacity will descend. [18] I will thank the LORD according to his righteousness; and I will praise the name of God Most

Superscript

New American Standard 1995	Hebrew
Psa. 7:0 A Shiggaion of David, which he sang to the LORD concerning Cush, a Benjamite.	שִׁגָּיוֹן לְדָוִד אֲשֶׁר־שָׁר לַיהוָה עַל־דִּבְרֵי־כוּשׁ בֶּן־יְמִינִי׃

Verse Analysis

This Psalm is dedicated to King Saul, whom David considered his most challenging enemy. David could have acted out in his anger but did not because the LORD anointed Saul. David respected the LORD and could not harm the LORD's anointed.

This Psalm is used as the "song of the day" on Purim.

שִׁגָּיוֹן (sheegion) – has two possible meanings. It can be translated as an "intellectual error." It was also considered a musical instrument used in the Levite Orchestra.

If one believes in the LORD, then one must be patient to wait for the final coming of justice. David was threatened by ruthless persecution and undeserved slander from Saul.

The tribe of Benjamin was considered the noblest tribe.

This is a psalm David wrote to celebrate Saul's downfall.

Verse Rewrite Emphasizing Spiritual Awareness

A mistake of David, a song he sang to the LORD concerning a Chushite descended from Benjamin.

Verse One

New American Standard 1995	Hebrew
Psa. 7:1 O LORD my God, in You I have taken refuge; Save me from all those who pursue me, and deliver me,	יְהוָה אֱלֹהַי בְּךָ חָסִיתִי הוֹשִׁיעֵנִי מִכָּל־רֹדְפַי וְהַצִּילֵנִי׃

Verse Rewrite Emphasizing Spiritual Awareness

LORD, my God, I have put my trust in you; save me from Saul and my enemies.

Verse Two

New American Standard 1995	Hebrew
2 Or he will tear my soul like a lion, Dragging me away, while there is none to deliver.	3 פֶּן־יִטְרֹף כְּאַרְיֵה נַפְשִׁי פֹּרֵק וְאֵין מַצִּיל׃

Verse Analysis

פֹּרֵק (porak) – means a forcible separation of things that hitherto had been linked together.

Metzudas David translated this verse as "if you will not save the enemy may it overcome me and rip me to pieces as a lion its prey."

Verse Rewrite Emphasizing Spiritual Awareness

Do not let my enemies tear me apart like a lion can, thus dismembering me without a rescuer.

New American Standard 1995	Hebrew

Psa. 7:3   O LORD my God, if I have done this,
    If there is injustice in my hands,
4   If I have rewarded evil to my friend,
    Or have plundered him who without cause was my adversary,
	יְהוָה אֱלֹהַי אִם־עָשִׂיתִי זֹאת
	
	אִם־יֶשׁ־עָוֶל בְּכַפָּי׃ ⁵
	
	גָּמַלְתִּי שׁוֹלְמִי רָע וָאֲחַלְּצָה
	
	צוֹרְרִי רֵיקָם׃

Verse Analysis

David now proceeds to explain that he does not deserve to be abused and threatened by his enemies because he had never mistreated them. David brings to mind that he often had the upper hand over Saul, but he never exploited his opportunities unjustly. David proved his loyalty because he could have killed Saul, but he did not.

Verse Rewrite Emphasizing Spiritual Awareness

V. 3 – LORD, my God, if there is any injustice in my hands,

V. 4 – If I repaid my friend with evil, I joyously freed myself from pursuit by those who oppressed me.

Verse Five

New American Standard 1995	Hebrew
5 Let the enemy pursue my soul and overtake *it;* And let him trample my life down to the ground And lay my glory in the dust. Selah.	יִרַדֹּף אוֹיֵב ׀ נַפְשִׁי וְיַשֵּׂג וְיִרְמֹס לָאָרֶץ חַיָּי וּכְבוֹדִי ׀ לֶעָפָר יַשְׁכֵּן סֶלָה׃

Verse Analysis

David knew that his soul would not be buried in the dirt of the Earth. He was speaking about the punishments that he may have deserved according to the distorted image of himself that his enemies had created.

Meditate upon this verse. (Selah – tradition says that this word means to meditate on the words.)

Verse Rewrite Emphasizing Spiritual Awareness

If I am guilty of wrongdoing, then let my enemies overtake me, end my life, and let my soul be lost in the dirt of the Earth. I will meditate upon these words.

Verse Six

New American Standard 1995	Hebrew
Psa. 7:6 Arise, O LORD, in Your anger; Lift up Yourself against the rage of my adversaries, And arouse Yourself for me; You have appointed judgment.	קוּמָה יְהוָה ׀ בְּאַפֶּךָ הִנָּשֵׂא בְּעַבְרוֹת צוֹרְרָי וְעוּרָה אֵלַי מִשְׁפָּט צִוִּיתָ׃

Verse Analysis

The appointed judgment is a universal judgment that has been proclaimed against the nations of the world, as said in Deuteronomy 32:41.

> **41**   If I sharpen My flashing sword,
> And My hand takes hold on justice,
> I will render vengeance on My adversaries,
> And I will repay those who hate Me.

Verse Rewrite Emphasizing Spiritual Awareness

Rise LORD in your anger, lift Yourself up in a fury against my tormentors, and strengthen me to mete out the judgment You commanded.

Verse Seven

New American Standard 1995	Hebrew
7 Let the assembly of the peoples encompass You, And over them return on high.	וַעֲדַת לְאֻמִּים תְּסוֹבְבֶךָּ וְעָלֶיהָ לַמָּרוֹם שׁוּבָה׃

Verse Analysis

This verse is referring to the universal judgment, which shall proclaim the LORD's sovereignty. The knowledge of the LORD will be spread over the nations, and they will gather together as one congregation.

Ibn Ezra said that when the assembly of nations surrounded David, it was as if they surrounded the LORD. David was the LORD's faithful servant, and the LORD's presence followed him wherever he went.

Verse Rewrite Emphasizing Spiritual Awareness

So the nations that surround the LORD will gather together as one congregation as you return to your heaven.

Verse Eight

New American Standard 1995	Hebrew
8 The LORD judges the peoples; Vindicate me, O LORD, according to my righteousness and my integrity that is in me.	יְהוָה֮ יָדִ֪ין עַ֫מִּ֥ים שָׁפְטֵ֥נִי יְהוָ֑ה כְּצִדְקִ֥י וּכְתֻמִּ֖י עָלָֽי׃

Verse Analysis

יָדִ֪ין - (yadeen) – means "to judge." This word denotes the application of judgment to one individual. Judgment comes from the Sefirot Gevurah.

Radak describes the nations as the tribes of Israel who were hostile to David. David did not want the bulk of the people to be punished. He only wanted the ones that were plotting against him punished.

Verse Rewrite Emphasizing Spiritual Awareness

The LORD will judge the nations and tribes who are against me one day. Judge me (David) also according to my righteousness and integrity.

Verse Nine

New American Standard 1995	Hebrew
[9] O let the evil of the wicked come to an end, but establish the righteous; For the righteous God tries the hearts and minds.	יִגְמָר־נָא רַע ׀ רְשָׁעִים֮ וּתְכוֹנֵן צַדִּיק וּבֹחֵן לִבּוֹת וּכְלָיוֹת אֱלֹהִים צַדִּיק׃

Verse Analysis

The LORD tests our moral aspirations and our physical desires by causing suffering. These trials are meant to purify us, which increases our moral strength and resolution, and which, therefore, more than compensates us. Gevurah ensures that justice is offered to the wicked as well as to the righteous.

David's prayer is for the evil of the wicked to disappear. He is not praying for the wicked to die.

Verse Rewrite Emphasizing Spiritual Awareness

Let the evil that the wicked perform be vanquished, and sustain the righteous whose hearts and minds are pure.

Verse Ten

New American Standard 1995	Hebrew
10 My shield is with God, Who saves the upright in heart.	מָֽגִנִּ֥י עַל־אֱלֹהִ֑ים מ֝וֹשִׁ֗יעַ יִשְׁרֵי־לֵֽב׃

Verse Analysis

The LORD helps those who remain upright in their thoughts and actions.

Verse Rewrite Emphasizing Spiritual Awareness

The LORD is my shield who saves the upright in heart.

Verse Eleven

New American Standard 1995	Hebrew
¹¹ God is a righteous judge, And a God who has indignation every day.	אֱלֹהִים שׁוֹפֵט צַדִּיק וְאֵל זֹעֵם בְּכָל־יוֹם

Verse Analysis

The LORD will not wait until the Tikkun (Great Judgment day), when all evil will disappear. The wicked will sense the LORD's anger from their evil every day.

Verse Rewrite Emphasizing Spiritual Awareness

The LORD is a righteous judge who makes his indignation against the wicked known every day.

Verse Twelve

New American Standard 1995	Hebrew
Psa. 7:12　　　If a man does not repent, He will sharpen His sword; 　　　He has bent His bow and made it ready.	אִם־לֹא יָשׁוּב חַרְבּוֹ יִלְטוֹשׁ קַשְׁתּוֹ דָרַךְ וַיְכוֹנְנֶהָ׃

Verse Analysis

The subject of this verse is a reference to the person whom the LORD makes His indignation felt every day.

The Sage Rashi said that this verse refers to the LORD preparing His "weapons" to punish the stubborn sinner if he does not repent.

Verse Rewrite Emphasizing Spiritual Awareness

If a person does not return to the LORD (repent), then the LORD will prepare His weapons to be used against the sinner.

<h1>Verse Thirteen</h1>

New American Standard 1995	Hebrew
13 He has also prepared ¹for Himself deadly weapons; He makes His arrows fiery shafts.	וְ֭לוֹ הֵכִ֣ין כְּלֵי־מָ֑וֶת חִ֝צָּ֗יו לְֽדֹלְקִ֥ים יִפְעָֽל׃

<h2>Verse Analysis</h2>

This verse is a verse of parallelism with the previous verse.

<h2>Verse Rewrite Emphasizing Spiritual Awareness</h2>

The LORD prepared His deadly weapons against the sinners.

Verse Fourteen

New American Standard 1995	Hebrew
14 Behold, he travails with wickedness, And he conceives mischief and brings forth falsehood.	הִנֵּה יְחַבֶּל־אָוֶן וְהָרָה עָמָל וְיָלַד שָׁקֶר׃

Verse Analysis

He who sows devotion to duty will reap the wages of truth.

Verse Rewrite Emphasizing Spiritual Awareness

Behold, he travails with wickedness, and conceives mischief, and brings forth falsehood.

Verse Fifteen

New American Standard 1995	Hebrew
15 He has dug a pit and hollowed it out, And has fallen into the hole which he made.	בּוֹר כָּרָה וַיַּחְפְּרֵהוּ וַיִּפֹּל בְּשַׁחַת יִפְעָל׃

Verse Analysis

The person who conceived of the previous verse's inequity created a snare that he/she fell into. The hollowed-out pit is a metaphor for the conceived sinful act.

Verse Rewrite Emphasizing Spiritual Awareness

He has dug a pit and has hallowed it, and then he fell into the pit which he had prepared.

Verse Sixteen

New American Standard 1995	Hebrew
16 His mischief will return upon his own head, And his violence will descend upon his own pate.	יָשׁוּב עֲמָלוֹ בְרֹאשׁוֹ וְעַל קָדְקֳדוֹ חֲמָסוֹ יֵרֵד׃

Verse Analysis

עָמֵל ('āmēl) – which means "toiling."

"The verb עָמַל is one of several Hebrew verbs for "labor, work, toil." Other major terms include עָבַד "to work, serve," and עָצָה "to make, do, work" (both of which see). עָמַל is used less often than those two verbs, and is employed often with the nuance of the drudgery of toil rather than the nobility of labor. Hebrew עָמַל is cognate to Arabic *'amila* "to labor," and to the Akkadian noun *nīmēlu*, that produced by work, "gain, possessions."

The root עָמַל relates to the dark side of labor, the grievous and unfulfilling aspect of work. A biblical view of labor based on this word alone would be defective, but this aspect of work should be included in a full induction. Thus Moses uses this term to describe the frustration and struggle of the worker in this ephemeral, transitory world (Ps 90:10). No wonder he cries out to the eternal God "and let thy beauty (eternal, lovely work) be upon us" (v. 17). The root in its several forms is used especially by Solomon in Eccl as he details the frustration, profitlessness, and transitory (הֶבֶל) benefits of day-by-day labor; such is noted when that labor is not seen as service (even worship!) to God, but simply as work done "under the sun." For the man whose relationship to God is tenuous, there is no profit (יִתְרוֹן) from all his work (Eccl 1:3). Yet even in Eccl there are glimpses of a higher view of labor: "every one who eats and drinks and sees good in all his labor-it is the gift of God"" Source: The Theological Wordbook of the Old Testament.

The Sage Malbim translates this word to mean "internal mental exertion to do evil."

Verse Rewrite Emphasizing Spiritual Awareness

His evil deeds will recoil upon his head, and upon his head will his violence descend.

Verse Seventeen

New American Standard 1995	Hebrew
Psa. 7:17 I will give thanks to the LORD according to His righteousness And will sing praise to the name of the LORD Most High.	אוֹדֶה יְהוָה כְּצִדְקוֹ וַאֲזַמְּרָה שֵׁם־יְהוָה עֶלְיוֹן׃

Verse Analysis

David acknowledged the fact that the LORD is indeed the LORD. David wants to pay homage with his righteousness to the LORD.

Verse Rewrite Emphasizing Spiritual Awareness

I will pay homage to the LORD in accordance with His righteousness and will always sing praises to the LORD's name.

Complete Psalm Rewrite Emphasizing Spiritual Awareness

A mistake of David, a song he sang to the LORD concerning a Chushite descended from Benjamin.

LORD, my God, I have put my trust in you; save me from Saul and my enemies.

V. 3 – LORD, my God, if there is any injustice in my hands,

V. 4 – If I repaid my friend with evil, I joyously freed myself from pursuit by those who oppressed me.

If I am guilty of wrongdoing, then let my enemies overtake me, end my life, and let my soul be lost in the dirt of the Earth. I will meditate upon these words.

Rise LORD in your anger, lift Yourself up in a fury against my tormentors, and strengthen me to mete out the judgment You commanded.

So the nations that surround the LORD will gather together as one congregation as you return to your heaven.

The LORD will judge the nations and tribes who are against me one day. Judge me (David) also according to my righteousness and integrity.

Let the evil that the wicked perform be vanquished, and sustain the righteous whose hearts and minds are pure.

The LORD is a righteous judge who makes his indignation against the wicked known every day.

If a person does not return to the LORD (repent), then the LORD will prepare His weapons to be used against the sinner.

The LORD prepared His deadly weapons against the sinners.

Behold, he travails with wickedness, and conceives mischief, and brings forth falsehood.

He has dug a pit and has hallowed it, and then he fell into the pit which he had prepared.

His evil deeds will recoil upon his head, and upon his head will his violence descend.

PSALM EIGHT

Lanugage

New American Standard 1995	Hebrew
[0] For the choir director; on the Gittith. A Psalm of David. [1] O LORD, our Lord, how majestic is Your name in all the earth, who have displayed Your splendor above the heavens! [2] From the mouth of infants and nursing babes You have established strength because of Your adversaries, to make the enemy and the revengeful cease. [3] When I consider Your heavens, the work of Your fingers, the moon and the stars, which You have ordained; [4] What is man that You take thought of him, and the son of man that You care for him? [5] Yet You have made him a little lower than God, and You crown him with glory and majesty! [6] You make him to rule over the works of Your hands; You have put all things under his feet, [7] All sheep and oxen, and also the beasts of the field, [8] The birds of the heavens and the fish of the sea, whatever passes through the paths of the seas. [9] O LORD, our Lord, how majestic is Your name in all the earth!	לַמְנַצֵּחַ עַל־הַגִּתִּית מִזְמוֹר [1] לְדָוִד ׃ [2] יְהוָה אֲדֹנֵינוּ מָה־ אַדִּיר שִׁמְךָ בְּכָל־הָאָרֶץ אֲשֶׁר תְּנָה הוֹדְךָ עַל־ הַשָּׁמָיִם ׃ [3] מִפִּי עוֹלְלִים ׀ וְיֹנְקִים יִסַּדְתָּ עֹז לְמַעַן צוֹרְרֶיךָ לְהַשְׁבִּית אוֹיֵב וּמִתְנַקֵּם ׃ [4] כִּי־אֶרְאֶה שָׁמֶיךָ מַעֲשֵׂי אֶצְבְּעֹתֶיךָ יָרֵחַ וְכוֹכָבִים אֲשֶׁר כּוֹנָנְתָּה ׃ [5] מָה־אֱנוֹשׁ כִּי־תִזְכְּרֶנּוּ וּבֶן־ אָדָם כִּי תִפְקְדֶנּוּ ׃ [6] וַתְּחַסְּרֵהוּ מְּעַט מֵאֱלֹהִים וְכָבוֹד וְהָדָר תְּעַטְּרֵהוּ ׃ [7] תַּמְשִׁילֵהוּ בְּמַעֲשֵׂי יָדֶיךָ כֹּל שַׁתָּה תַחַת־רַגְלָיו ׃ [8] צֹנֶה וַאֲלָפִים כֻּלָּם וְגַם בַּהֲמוֹת

	שָׂדָי ׃ ⁹ צִפּוֹר שָׁמַיִם וּדְגֵי הַיָּם עֹבֵר אָרְחוֹת יַמִּים ׃ ¹⁰ יְהוָה אֲדֹנֵינוּ מָה־אַדִּיר שִׁמְךָ בְּכָל־הָאָרֶץ ׃

Psa. 8:1 For praise, on the lyre that he brought from Gath. A hymn of David. [2] O God our master, how lofty is your name and praiseworthy in all the earth, you who have placed your splendor above the heavens. [3] From the mouth of children and infants you have established strength because of your oppressors, to bring to naught the enemy and the violent man. [4] Because I see your heavens, the works of your fingers, the moon and the stars that you have fixed in place, [5] What is a son of man, because you will remember his deeds, and a son of man, because you will punish him? [6] And you have made him a little less than the angels, and you will crown him with glory and brightness. [7] You made him ruler over the works of your hands; all things you have placed under his feet. [8] Sheep and oxen, all of them, and also the beasts of the field. [9] The birds of the air, and the fish of the sea, and Leviathan, who passes along the paths of the sea. [10] O God our master, how lofty and praiseworthy is your name in all the earth!

Superscript

New American Standard 1995	Hebrew
[0] For the choir director; on the Gittith. A Psalm of David.	לַמְנַצֵּחַ עַל־הַגִּתִּית מִזְמוֹר לְדָוִד׃ [1]

Verse Analysis

גִּתִּית (gittît) The Theological Wordbook of the Old Testament indicates that the meaning of the word is unknown and is probably a musical instrument. This word can mean "winepress." It is an allegorical expression for the grievous catastrophe which the LORD had visited upon the nations. It alludes to Israel's enemies who are destined to be crushed by the LORD like grapes in a winepress. The winepress does not wholly destroy the grape. Instead, it removes the fine and noble essence which was locked within it. This word may refer to a special kind of musical instrument.

Verse Rewrite Emphasizing Spiritual Awareness

To the Sefirah Netzach, the Sefirah of Victory who gives triumph over one's enemies.

Verse One

New American Standard 1995	Hebrew
[1] O LORD, our Lord, how majestic is Your name in all the earth, who have displayed your splendor above the heavens!	יְהוָה אֲדֹנֵינוּ מָה־אַדִּיר שִׁמְךָ בְּכָל־הָאָרֶץ

Verse Analysis

The universal knowledge of Adonai is to be spread over the Earth. It is the power of the LORD.

עַל־הַשָּׁמָיִם (al hashamaym). This means "over the heavens." The Zohar says that the LORD is in Heaven's eighth layer when He is not on the throne in the seventh layer. The eighth layer is considered above Heaven.

יְהוָה (pronounced Adonai). The Sage Malbim called this the name of perpetual bringing forth into existence, for it is with this name that the LORD reveals himself to us utilizing all the creations which He brought out into the visible world.

שִׁמְךָ (sheem'cha). This means "your name." The Sage Radak said that the LORD's name is Himself, and He Himself is His name.

Verse Rewrite Emphasizing Spiritual Awareness

LORD, Your mighty Name must be told to all people of the Earth even when You are in the eighth layer of Heaven.

Verse Two

New American Standard 1995	Hebrew
² From the mouth of infants and nursing babes you have established strength because of Your adversaries, to make the enemy and the revengeful cease.	³ מִפִּי עוֹלְלִים וְיֹנְקִים יִסַּדְתָּ עֹז לְמַעַן צוֹרְרֶיךָ לְהַשְׁבִּית אוֹיֵב וּמִתְנַקֵּם:

Verse Analysis

מִפִּי עוֹלְלִים (meephee ol' lym). This phrase means "from a child's mouth." Allegorically it means that if recognizing the LORD was difficult beyond human ability, it would take more than just studying His Word.

Even if humans forget the LORD's name it can never be erased from the Scripture.

The LORD's name is written in the Heavens and away from human hands but still intelligible to children. Without the knowledge of the LORD, humans would only pursue their happiness and not care for others.

Verse Rewrite Emphasizing Spiritual Awareness

Even children will understand who the LORD is. Your foes will never banish your Name.

Verse Three & Four

New American Standard 1995	Hebrew
³ When I consider Your heavens, the work of Your fingers, the moon and the stars, which You have ordained; ⁴ What is man that You take thought of him, and the son of man that You care for him?	⁴ כִּי־אֶרְאֶה שָׁמֶיךָ מַעֲשֵׂי אֶצְבְּעֹתֶיךָ יָרֵחַ וְכוֹכָבִים אֲשֶׁר כּוֹנָנְתָּה׃ ⁵ מָה־אֱנוֹשׁ כִּי־תִזְכְּרֶנּוּ וּבֶן־אָדָם כִּי תִפְקְדֶנּוּ׃

Verse Analysis

Every star is a separate, unique, individual sphere in the Universe. This Psalm is uttered at the sight of the starry sky at night.

אָדָם (adam). This word means "man, mankind," and the first human's name that the LORD created. The word denotes the pure human, the representative of the LORD on Earth. His task is to realize the moral purposes for which the LORD has called the physical world into being.

An "adam" knows only his duty, seeks justification of his desires and ambition.

אֱנוֹשׁ (enosh). This word means "man, mortal man, person." When this word is used, it refers to the weaknesses, fragility, and limitations imposed upon human's nature.

David wondered why the LORD made him so frail when he was made in the LORD's image and placed him on the Earth to represent divine sovereignty.

Verse Rewrite Emphasizing Spiritual Awareness

v. 3 – When I behold the stars in Heaven, the work of your fingers, the luminaries that you have given to each task.

v. 4 – Humans are frail, yet LORD, you remember us, and what of the children of humans that you think about us.

Verse Five

New American Standard 1995	Hebrew
[5] Yet You have made him a little lower than God, and You crown him with glory and majesty!	[6] וַתְּחַסְּרֵהוּ מְּעַט מֵאֱלֹהִים וְכָבוֹד וְהָדָר תְּעַטְּרֵהוּ :

Verse Analysis

Humans are the first servants of the LORD because humans are the only creatures called upon to do their duty, morally free consciously, the only being so endowed besides the LORD, that one and absolute free force.

Despite human fragility, the LORD made humans a bit lower than the angels

Verse Rewrite Emphasizing Spiritual Awareness

LORD, you made us a little less than the angels, giving humans a soul to crown him/her with honor and dignity.

Verse Six

New American Standard 1995	Hebrew
[6] You make him to rule over the works of Your hands; You have put all things under his feet,	תַּמְשִׁילֵהוּ בְּמַעֲשֵׂי יָדֶיךָ כֹּל שַׁתָּה תַחַת־ רַגְלָיו׃ [7]

Verse Analysis

The Sage Radak said, by virtue of his exalted soul, humans were given mastery over the entire world. Humans must not enforce his/her own pride upon others. The LORD appointed humans as His stewards in the household of this terrestrial world to fulfill His purpose. Man's purpose is to be good stewards of the Earth.

Verse Rewrite Emphasizing Spiritual Awareness

You made humans the stewards of your creation and placed everything under them.

Verse Seven

New American Standard 1995	Hebrew
[7] All sheep and oxen, and also the beasts of the field,	צֹנֶה וַאֲלָפִים כֻּלָּם וְגַם בַּהֲמוֹת שָׂדָי: [8]

Verse Analysis

Sheep are animals that need constant protection by humans and need humans to build shelters for them.

Cattle are animals that assume leadership in the herd by virtue of their superior strength and larger size.

Verse Rewrite Emphasizing Spiritual Awareness

Sheep and cattle, even the beasts of the fields,

<h1 style="text-align:center">Verse Eight</h1>

New American Standard 1995	Hebrew
[8] The birds of the heavens and the fish of the sea, whatever passes through the paths of the seas.	צִפּוֹר שָׁמַיִם וּדְגֵי הַיָּם עֹבֵר אָרְחוֹת יַמִּים׃ [9]

Verse Analysis

This verse is a metaphor for a movement with a specific goal.

Verse Rewrite Emphasizing Spiritual Awareness

The birds of the sky and the fish of the sea; for he crosses over the paths of the seas.

Verse Nine

New American Standard 1995	Hebrew
[9] O LORD, our Lord, how majestic is Your name in all the earth!	[10] יְהוָה אֲדֹנֵינוּ מָה־אַדִּיר שִׁמְךָ בְּכָל־הָאָרֶץ׃

Verse Analysis

Humans should have a life of service to the LORD.

Verse Rewrite Emphasizing Spiritual Awareness

LORD, your name is mighty throughout the Earth.

To the Sefirah Netzach, the Sefirah of Victory who gives triumph over one's enemies.

LORD, Your mighty Name must be told to all people of the Earth even when You are in the eighth layer of Heaven.

Even children will understand who the LORD is. Your foes will never banish your Name.

When I behold the stars in Heaven, the work of your fingers, the luminaries that you have given to each task.

Humans are frail, yet LORD, you remember us, and what of the children of humans that you think about us.

LORD, you made us a little less than the angels, giving humans a soul to crown him/her with honor and dignity.

You made humans the stewards of your creation and placed everything under them. Sheep and cattle, even the beasts of the fields,

The birds of the sky and the fish of the sea; for he crosses over the paths of the seas.

LORD, your name is mighty throughout the Earth.

Language

New American Standard 1995	Hebrew
0 For the choir director; on Muthlabben. A Psalm of David. **1** I will give thanks to the LORD with all my heart; I will tell of all Your wonders. **2** I will be glad and exult in You; I will sing praise to Your name, O Most High. **3** When my enemies turn back, They stumble and perish before You. **4** For You have maintained my just cause; You have sat on the throne judging righteously. **5** You have rebuked the nations, You have destroyed the wicked; You have blotted out their name forever and ever. **6** The enemy has come to an end in perpetual ruins, And You have uprooted the cities; The very memory of them has perished. **7** But the LORD abides forever; He has established His throne for judgment, **8** And He will judge the world in righteousness; He will execute judgment for the peoples with equity. **9** The LORD also will be a stronghold for the oppressed, A stronghold in times of trouble; **10** And those who know Your name will put their trust in You, For You, O LORD, have not forsaken those who seek You.	9:1 . לַמְנַצֵּחַ עַלְמוּת לַבֵּן מִזְמוֹר לְדָוִד : 2 אוֹדֶה יְהוָה בְּכָל־לִבִּי 3 : אֲסַפְּרָה כָּל־נִפְלְאוֹתֶיךָ אֶשְׂמְחָה וְאֶעֶלְצָה בָךְ אֲזַמְּרָה שִׁמְךָ עֶלְיוֹן : 4 בְּשׁוּב־אוֹיְבַי 5 : אָחוֹר יִכָּשְׁלוּ וְיֹאבְדוּ מִפָּנֶיךָ כִּי־עָשִׂיתָ מִשְׁפָּטִי וְדִינִי יָשַׁבְתָּ לְכִסֵּא שׁוֹפֵט צֶדֶק : 6 גָּעַרְתָּ גוֹיִם אִבַּדְתָּ רָשָׁע שְׁמָם מָחִיתָ לְעוֹלָם וָעֶד : 7 הָאוֹיֵב תַּמּוּ חֳרָבוֹת לָנֶצַח וְעָרִים נָתַשְׁתָּ אָבַד זִכְרָם הֵמָּה : 8 וַיהוָה לְעוֹלָם יֵשֵׁב כּוֹנֵן לַמִּשְׁפָּט כִּסְאוֹ : 9 וְהוּא יִשְׁפֹּט־תֵּבֵל בְּצֶדֶק יָדִין לְאֻמִּים בְּמֵישָׁרִים : 10 וִיהִי יְהוָה מִשְׂגָּב לַדָּךְ מִשְׂגָּב לְעִתּוֹת בַּצָּרָה : 11 וְיִבְטְחוּ בְךָ יוֹדְעֵי שְׁמֶךָ כִּי לֹא־עָזַבְתָּ דֹרְשֶׁיךָ יְהוָה : 12 זַמְּרוּ לַיהוָה יֹשֵׁב צִיּוֹן הַגִּידוּ בָעַמִּים

¹¹ Sing praises to the LORD, who dwells in Zion; Declare among the peoples His deeds.

¹² For He who requires blood remembers them; He does not forget the cry of the afflicted.

¹³ Be gracious to me, O LORD; See my affliction from those who hate me, You who lift me up from the gates of death,

¹⁴ That I may tell of all Your praises, That in the gates of the daughter of Zion I may rejoice in Your salvation.

¹⁵ The nations have sunk down in the pit which they have made; In the net which they hid, their own foot has been caught.

¹⁶ The LORD has made Himself known; He has executed judgment. In the work of his own hands the wicked is snared. Higgaion Selah.

¹⁷ The wicked will return to Sheol, Even all the nations who forget God.

¹⁸ For the needy will not always be forgotten, Nor the hope of the afflicted perish forever.

¹⁹ Arise, O LORD, do not let man prevail; Let the nations be judged before You.

²⁰ Put them in fear, O LORD; Let the nations know that they are but men. Selah.

עֲלִילוֹתָיו ׃ ¹³ כִּי־דֹרֵשׁ דָּמִים אוֹתָם זָכָר לֹא־שָׁכַח צַעֲקַת עֲנִיִּים [עֲנָוִים ׃] ¹⁴ חָנְנֵנִי יְהוָה רְאֵה עָנְיִי מִשֹּׂנְאָי מְרוֹמְמִי מִשַּׁעֲרֵי מָוֶת ׃ ¹⁵ לְמַעַן אֲסַפְּרָה כָּל־תְּהִלָּתֶיךָ בְּשַׁעֲרֵי בַת־צִיּוֹן אָגִילָה בִּישׁוּעָתֶךָ ׃ ¹⁶ טָבְעוּ גוֹיִם בְּשַׁחַת עָשׂוּ בְּרֶשֶׁת־זוּ טָמָנוּ נִלְכְּדָה רַגְלָם ׃ ¹⁷ נוֹדַע | יְהוָה מִשְׁפָּט עָשָׂה בְּפֹעַל כַּפָּיו נוֹקֵשׁ רָשָׁע הִגָּיוֹן סֶלָה ׃ ¹⁸ יָשׁוּבוּ רְשָׁעִים לִשְׁאוֹלָה כָּל־גּוֹיִם שְׁכֵחֵי אֱלֹהִים ׃ ¹⁹ כִּי לֹא לָנֶצַח יִשָּׁכַח אֶבְיוֹן תִּקְוַת עֲנָוִים [עֲנִיִּים] תֹּאבַד לָעַד ׃ ²⁰ קוּמָה יְהוָה אַל־יָעֹז אֱנוֹשׁ יִשָּׁפְטוּ גוֹיִם עַל־פָּנֶיךָ ׃ ²¹ שִׁיתָה יְהוָה | מוֹרָה לָהֶם יֵדְעוּ גוֹיִם אֱנוֹשׁ הֵמָּה סֶּלָה ׃

[1] For praise, concerning the death of the man who went out between the armies. A hymn of David. [ANOTHER TARGUM: For praise, concerning the sweetness of the sound by a son. A hymn of David.] [2] I will sing praise in the LORD's presence with all my heart; I will tell all of your miracles. [3] I will be glad and rejoice in your word; I will praise your name, O Most High. [4] When my enemies turn back, they will stumble and perish before you. [5] Because you have accomplished my vindication and my judgment; you sat down on the throne of the righteous judge. [6] You rebuked the peoples of the Philistines; you destroyed Goliath the wicked; their name you erased forever and ever. [7] And when the enemy fell, his forces were obliterated, and their fortresses were laid waste forever, and as for their cities, you destroyed the memory of them forever. [8] But as for the word of the LORD, his seat is in the highest heaven forever; he has established his throne for judgment. [9] And he shall judge the people of the earth in righteousness; he will judge the Gentiles in uprightness. [10] And the word of the LORD will be strength to the poor, strength in times of distress. [11] And those who know your name will look at your hope , because you have not abandoned those who seek you, O LORD. [12] Sing praise before the LORD who made his presence rest in Zion; tell his deeds among the Gentiles. [13] For he avenges the innocent blood; he remembers the, he does not neglect the complaint of the humble. [14] Pity me, O LORD; see my pain caused by my enemies , you who lift me up from the entrances of death. [15] So that I may tell all your praises in the entrances of the gates of the assembly of Zion; I will exult in your redemption. [16] The peoples have sunk in the pit that they made; in the very net they concealed, their feet are caught. [17] Manifest before the LORD is the judgement he executed: through the works of his hands, the wicked man stumbled, the righteous will rejoice forever. [18] The wicked will return to Sheol, all the Gentiles who neglected the fear of the LORD. [19] For the needy man is not forever neglected; the hope of the humble will not perish forever. [20] Arise, O LORD, may the wicked son of man not grow strong, may the Gentiles be judged in your presence. [21] Put, O LORD, fear on them; let the peoples know that they are a son of man forever.

Superscript

New American Standard 1995	Hebrew
[0] For the choir director; on Muth-labben. A Psalm of David.	לַמְנַצֵּחַ עַלְמוּת לַבֵּן מִזְמוֹר לְדָוִד

Superscript Analysis

עַלְמוּת לַבֵּן (al'mut laben) – means "on the death of the son." In several Hebrew versions of this Psalm, this phrase is written עַל־מוּת לַבֵּן which corresponds to the actual translation. The WTT version connects *al* and *mut*. This is because the Sages do not believe that the translation "on the death of the son" fits this phrase. This Psalm does not talk about death. The Sage Rashi observed that since the Psalm does not indicate death, the phrase must mean something else. This superscript could be saying that immortality will be given to Israel because Israel is the only nation that submitted willingly to the guidance of the LORD and acceptance of His Torah.

The Psalm addresses the nation of Israel and not an individual. *Laben* refers to Israel's relationship to the LORD.

The Psalm expresses the historical events of Israel during their wanderings among the peoples of the world. Throughout Israel's history, it has suffered trials and tribulations. Larger nations have left a trail of ruins upon their paths to military victories, and it was Israel who suffered at their hands.

Verse Rewrite Emphasizing Spiritual Awareness

To the LORD, who grants Netzach in the form of immortality to the nation of Israel. A psalm of David.

Verse One

New American Standard 1995	Hebrew
[1] I will give thanks to the LORD with all my heart; I will tell of all Your wonders.	2 אוֹדֶה יְהוָה בְּכָל־לִבִּי אֲסַפְּרָה כָּל־נִפְלְאוֹתֶיךָ

Verse Analysis

בְּכָל־לִבִּי (b'kal leebee) means "all my heart." The Psalmist is saying that we need to recognize the LORD with all our being. This act was considered a great miracle when Israel first became a nation, and the LORD revealed His greatness to them.

David's victory over Goliath was an important event in Israel's history, and because the LORD granted David victory, He deserves full-hearted praise.

A basic credo of Judaism is that one must praise the LORD in good and bad times. An appreciation for the LORD is necessary all the time.

Verse Rewrite Emphasizing Spiritual Awareness

I will always praise you, LORD, and tell the nations of your wondrous works in good and bad times.

Verse Two

New American Standard 1995	Hebrew
2 I will be glad and exult in You; I will sing praise to Your name, O Most High.	אֶשְׂמְחָה וְאֶעֶלְצָה בָךְ אֲזַמְּרָה 3 : שִׁמְךָ עֶלְיוֹן :

Verse Analysis

אֶשְׂמְחָה (as'm'cha) means "to rejoice." This is a frame of mind that can recognize that which is good and true. One comes closer to the LORD through duty fulfilled.

Exulting the LORD gave David confidence when he faced Goliath. Therefore, if one exalts the LORD, one will gain confidence in everything that life offers.

Verse Rewrite Emphasizing Spiritual Awareness

I rejoice and sing praises to your name, O most high.

Verse Three

New American Standard 1995	Hebrew
3 When my enemies turn back, They stumble and perish before You.	4 בְּשׁוּב־אוֹיְבַי אָחוֹר יִכָּשְׁלוּ וְיֹאבְדוּ מִפָּנֶיךָ

Verse Analysis

When the Philistines retreated after David slew Goliath, the Psalmist said that they stumbled and crawled back to their homeland. When David beat Goliath, it was not the power of David which prevailed; it was the power of the LORD through David, which prevailed. The Philistines saw the power and might of the LORD through David.

Verse Rewrite Emphasizing Spiritual Awareness

When Goliath was slain, the Philistines stumbled back home because they were in fear of Gevurah. Justice for Israel was being served because of the Philistines oppression.

Verse Four

New American Standard 1995	Hebrew
[4] For You have maintained my just cause; You have sat on the throne judging righteously.	כִּי־עָשִׂיתָ מִשְׁפָּטִי וְדִינִי יָשַׁבְתָּ לְכִסֵּא שׁוֹפֵט צֶדֶק׃

Verse Analysis

Israel's nation was dependent solely upon the spiritual perception of truth and the honorable discharge of life's duties, all subordinated to the LORD. The nations that surrounded Israel were opposed to them because they were based on materialism. Therefore, Israel represents the spiritual world in Malkhut. In contrast, the rest of the nations of the world represent the material world in Malkhut. Only in Malkhut can the spiritual and material world connect.

Every time a kingdom is built, which neglects moral Law and is based on violence, it eventually crumbles and perishes. When a nation's goal is material possessions, it will not last the test of time. Israel depended on the LORD, which brought them into a spiritual connection with the LORD.

When Goliath met David on the battlefield, he cursed the name of the LORD. The LORD sent Gevurah to execute justice on Goliath and the Philistines. People today need to learn the lesson of the Philistines. When the material world is more important than the spiritual world, Gevurah will reject them when learning Malkhut and entering Yesod. Materialistic people who ignore the LORD do not have a place in the Tree of Life.

Verse Rewrite Emphasizing Spiritual Awareness

You have furthered my destiny and appointed Gevruah to bring the judgment seat for judging righteously.

Verse Five

New American Standard 1995	Hebrew
5 You have rebuked the nations, You have destroyed the wicked; You have blotted out their name forever and ever.	6 גָּעַרְתָּ גוֹיִם אִבַּדְתָּ רָשָׁע שְׁמָם מָחִיתָ לְעוֹלָם וָעֶד :

Verse Analysis

When the LORD strikes down a lawless kingdom, it is a warning to the rest of the world's kingdoms to leave their evil. Immoral kingdoms will be destroyed b the LORD if they do not destroy themselves because of their wickedness. The Psalmist could also be talking about what was going to happen to Israel when she decided to stop following the Torah's moral Law and became like the nations that surrounded her. Israel must always survive because of the LORD's promise to Abraham.

Verse Rewrite Emphasizing Spiritual Awareness

For you have told the nations of the world that lawlessness and immorality will eventually bring Gevurah to the nation, and the nation will be erased from history.

Verse Six

New American Standard 1995	Hebrew
6 The enemy has come to an end in perpetual ruins, And You have uprooted the cities; The very memory of them has perished.	‏הָאוֹיֵב ׀ תַּמּוּ חֳרָבוֹת לָנֶצַח 7 וְעָרִים נָתַשְׁתָּ אָבַד זִכְרָם הֵמָּה׃

Verse Analysis

When a nation or kingdom is destroyed, it is generally erased from history. David continues to talk about the end of kingdoms that have been immoral. The memory of the wicked nations perishes overtime.

Verse Rewrite Emphasizing Spiritual Awareness

The enemy's kingdom has come to an end forever. You destroyed their cities, and they have been removed from history and thus forgotten.

Verse Seven

New American Standard 1995	Hebrew
7 But the LORD abides forever; He has established His throne for judgment,	8 וַיהוָה לְעוֹלָם יֵשֵׁב כּוֹנֵן לַמִּשְׁפָּט כִּסְאוֹ :

Verse Analysis

The LORD is resting until that future date when Gevurah's day of judgment arrives. The events of the world are preparations for said day. The Sage Rashi said that only after the eradication of Amalek the LORD's throne and name will be complete. The war against Amalek can be found in Exodus 17:16

> The LORD has sworn; the LORD will have war against Amalek from generation to generation. (Exodus 17:16)

Verse Rewrite Emphasizing Spiritual Awareness

The LORD is resting until the defeat of Amalek, for when that happens, Gevurah will judge the world from His throne.

Verse Eight

New American Standard 1995	Hebrew
[8] And He will judge the world in righteousness; He will execute judgment for the peoples with equity	וְהוּא יִשְׁפֹּט־תֵּבֵל בְּצֶדֶק יָדִין ׃ [9] לְאֻמִּים בְּמֵישָׁרִים ׃

Verse Analysis

וְהוּא יִשְׁפֹּט (v'hu yeesh'fot) – means "He will judge." This phrase denotes humankind's world, with all its chaos, following a stable course of development. One day the chaos of the world will be transformed into order by Gevurah (justice). Gevurah will bring justice by measuring all human affairs against the heavenly standard of justice.

If the world followed an international law founded upon mutual respect as the LORD demands, the outcome would be permanent peace on Earth.

Verse Rewrite Emphasizing Spiritual Awareness

And Gevurah will judge the world and will bring order to chaos through executing judgment upon the nations.

New American Standard 1995	Hebrew
[9] The LORD also will be a stronghold for the oppressed, A stronghold in times of trouble;	וִיהִי יְהוָה מִשְׂגָּב לַדָּךְ מִשְׂגָּב לְעִתּוֹת בַּצָּרָה׃

Verse Analysis

שָׁפַט (shapet) – means "to judge." "The primary sense of שָׁפַט is to exercise the processes of government. However, since the ancients did not always divide the functions of government, as most modern governments do, between legislative, executive, and judicial functions (and departments), the common translation, "to judge," misleads us. For, the word, judge, as שָׁפַט is usually translated, in modern English, means to exercise only the judicial function of government." (TWOT) It can also denote a high tower for the afflicted. The LORD will bring judgment against a government that oppresses its people.

Everything takes time to develop. At times the people of Israel wondered where the LORD was. Why did the LORD not help them? Sometimes it takes time for the LORD to react to injustice. This is because the LORD gives people time to repent.

When the LORD is ready for global judgment, He will correct the injustice that was done to Israel. The Sage Radak said that the moment of great distress was when the Philistines threatened to destroy Israel. The threat was the greatest during the battle when David killed Goliath.

Verse Rewrite Emphasizing Spiritual Awareness

The LORD shall become a high tower for the oppressed and afflicted and for those times of future distress.

Verse Ten

New American Standard 1995	Hebrew
[10] And those who know Your name will put their trust in You, For You, O LORD, have not forsaken those who seek You.	וַיִּבְטְחוּ בְךָ יוֹדְעֵי שְׁמֶךָ כִּי לֹא־[11] עָזַבְתָּ דֹרְשֶׁיךָ יְהוָה׃

Verse Analysis

Those who are being oppressed will wait patiently because they know the Name of the LORD. The people were sustained by the knowledge of His nature and His will. The people will not lose hope because they know the LORD is always with them and will bring justice.

Verse Rewrite Emphasizing Spiritual Awareness

The oppressed people who know the LORD's name shall always trust You; You have never forsaken all people who seek out your counsel and help for you.

Verse Eleven

New American Standard 1995	Hebrew
[11] Sing praises to the LORD, who dwells in Zion; Declare among the peoples His deeds.	זַמְּרוּ לַיהוָה יֹשֵׁב צִיּוֹן 12: הַגִּידוּ בָעַמִּים עֲלִילוֹתָיו:

Verse Analysis

The Temple of the LORD was built in Zion, and the people believed that the LORD dwelt there. The Shekinah lived in the Temple, the presence of the LORD. When the people sinned to the point when the LORD brought the Babylonians into Judah, He removed the Shekinah from the Temple. When that happened, the Babylonians destroyed the city and the Temple.

Verse Rewrite Emphasizing Spiritual Awareness

Sing praises to the LORD who dwells in the Temple in Zion, and declare His works among the nations.

Verse Twelve

New American Standard 1995	Hebrew
12 For He who requires blood remembers them; He does not forget the cry of the afflicted.	כִּי־דֹרֵשׁ דָּמִים אוֹתָם זָכָר לֹא־ שָׁכַח צַעֲקַת עֲנִיִּים [עֲנָוִים]׃

Verse Analysis

עֲנִיִּים [עֲנָוִים]׃ (aneeyeeym) (anaveem) – means "poor" and "humble." The word "poor" is misspelled in this Psalm, and the misspelled word means "humble." Hirsch said that this Psalm was written this way, with both words, to understand why the humble are made to suffer. The humble are dependent on higher powers and powerless to defend themselves. The humble were made to suffer to experience firsthand the pain of oppression by despots' heels. The despots should have learned that humane treatment is what the LORD wants for all people, especially Israel.

Verse Rewrite Emphasizing Spiritual Awareness

For the LORD, avenges blood has remembered them; He has not forgotten the cry of the humble.

Verse Thirteen

New American Standard 1995	Hebrew
13 Be gracious to me, O LORD; See my affliction from those who hate me, You who lift me up from the gates of death,	14 חָנְנֵנִי יְהוָה רְאֵה עָנְיִי מִשֹּׂנְאָי מְרוֹמְמִי מִשַּׁעֲרֵי מָוֶת׃

Verse Analysis

The first word is unique in that it has three נ in it. The word comes from the word חָנַן

(ḥānan), which means "to be gracious; to show pity." The Sage Alshich explained that the three *nun* letters are unusual. It shows that David asked the LORD for a generous portion of mercy.

Verse Rewrite Emphasizing Spiritual Awareness

Favor me, LORD. See my afflictions and give me a generous portion of mercy for you alone raise me above death's door.

Verse Fourteen

New American Standard 1995	Hebrew
[14] That I may tell of all Your praises, That in the gates of the daughter of Zion I may rejoice in Your salvation	15 לְמַ֫עַן אֲסַפְּרָ֗ה כָּל־תְּהִלָּתֶ֥יךָ בְּשַֽׁעֲרֵ֥י בַת־צִיּ֑וֹן אָ֝גִ֗ילָה בִּישׁוּעָתֶֽךָ׃

Verse Analysis

David said that when he is saved from his enemies, he will go to the gates of Zion to offer his thanksgiving because that is where the Shekinah resides.

Verse Rewrite Emphasizing Spiritual Awareness

That I may tell of Your acts and that I may take one-day rejoice within the gates of Zion, so that I may rejoice in your salvation.

New American Standard 1995	Hebrew
[15] The nations have sunk down in the pit which they have made; In the net which they hid, their own foot has been caught. [16] The LORD has made Himself known; He has executed judgment. In the work of his own hands the wicked is snared. Higgaion Selah.	16 טָבְעוּ גוֹיִם בְּשַׁחַת עָשׂוּ בְּרֶשֶׁת־זוּ טָמָנוּ נִלְכְּדָה רַגְלָם׃ 17 נוֹדַע ׀ יְהוָה מִשְׁפָּט עָשָׂה בְּפֹעַל כַּפָּיו נוֹקֵשׁ רָשָׁע הִגָּיוֹן סֶלָה׃

Verse Analysis

We can see a sign of the LORD's judgment whenever a wicked person gets caught in the trap of his/her own treacherous tricks.

הִגָּיוֹן. (heegaryon) – "means "meditation, whispering, melody. "The noun הִגָּיוֹן refers to the music of a harp in Psalm 92:3. Possibly a musical notation is meant by the "Higgaion" in 9:16 [H 17], but "meditation" is an alternate interpretation." (TWOT)

Verse Rewrite Emphasizing Spiritual Awareness

V16 – Whenever a nation falls into their own evil pit, into the very snare they caught their foot in,

V17 – The LORD becomes known because He sends Gevurah to execute judgment. Meditate on these two verses.

Verse Seventeen

New American Standard 1995	Hebrew
¹⁷ The wicked will return to Sheol, *Even* all the nations who forget God.	יָשׁוּבוּ רְשָׁעִים לִשְׁאוֹלָה כָּל־ גוֹיִם שְׁכֵחֵי אֱלֹהִים׃

Verse Analysis

יָשׁוּבוּ רְשָׁעִים לִשְׁאוֹלָה (yashuvu reshaeem leesheola) – means "the wicked will return to Sheol." Hirsch said this is not what the verse is saying. The wicked returning to Sheol presupposes that they have been in the grave once before. Instead, it means "they shall retreat to Sheol." They will sink back from the heights that they have climbed back to Sheol. The word שְׁאוֹלָה is derived from the root word, שָׁאל which means "to demand back." The Ruach (spirit) of humans did not spring from the dust, and therefore it is not doomed to return to dust. Only the Nefesh (flesh) returns to the dust. The Ruach is destined to Sheol only if the Torah's moral Laws are exploited for material gains.

Gehinnom consists of seven layers. The lowest layer is Sheol. Therefore, persons can be in Gehinnom and rise up to the higher layers away from Sheol. However, they can also sink back down the layers. The Zohar says that the Ruachim who have committed unforgivable sins are sent to Sheol and can never leave that layer. The Ruachim that are sent to Gehinnom is allowed to repent of their sins. The LORD determines which level of Gehinnom the Ruach is sent to upon the death of the Nefesh. From there, the Ruach repents from sin and moves up the levels of Gehinnom until it leaves Gehinnom and enters the Lower Waters of Heaven.

Verse Rewrite Emphasizing Spiritual Awareness

All the nations that have not lived according to the LORD's moral laws will retreat through Gehinnom toward Sheol.

Verse Eighteen

New American Standard 1995	Hebrew
18 For the needy will not always be forgotten, Nor the hope of the afflicted perish forever.	19 כִּי לֹא לָנֶצַח יִשָּׁכַח אֶבְיֹון תִּקְוַת עֲנָוִים [עֲנִיִּים] תֹּאבַד לָעַד ׃

Verse Analysis

The oppressors of Israel have forgotten about the LORD because Israel was helpless to defend themselves and at the mercy of the oppressors' will. These nations are not concerned about what the LORD will do to them because the LORD's people are under their power. The Psalmist reminds us that the LORD will never forget the weak, especially Israel. The LORD will help Israel even before the coming of the day of final judgment.

Verse Rewrite Emphasizing Spiritual Awareness

For the pauper shall not eternally be forgotten, nor shall the hope of the oppressed perish.

Verse Nineteen

New American Standard 1995	Hebrew
[19] Arise, O LORD, do not let man prevail; Let the nations be judged before You.	‏20 קוּמָה יְהוָה אַל־יָעֹז אֱנוֹשׁ: יִשָּׁפְטוּ גוֹיִם עַל־פָּנֶיךָ:‏

Verse Analysis

The Psalmist calls out to the LORD, urging Him to warn the overbearing oppressors by intervening in history.

Verse Rewrite Emphasizing Spiritual Awareness

Arise LORD and do not let the oppressors prevail as you send Gevurah to intervene in their doing.

New American Standard 1995	Hebrew
²⁰ Put them in fear, O LORD; Let the nations know that they are but men. Selah.	שִׁיתָה יְהוָה ׀ מוֹרָה לָהֶם ²¹ : יֵדְעוּ גוֹיִם אֱנוֹשׁ הֵמָּה סֶּלָה :

Verse Analysis

The Psalmist is asking that a spiritual and moral seed be placed in their oppressors to teach them how to return to the paths of prudence and understanding. Israel did not pray that the nations who oppressed them should perish. They prayed that their oppressors would see the evil in their ways and would return to the LORD's moral code.

Verse Rewrite Emphasizing Spiritual Awareness

May the LORD teach and correct the nations who oppress Israel. May they stop their violence. Meditate on this verse.

Complete Psalm Rewrite Emphasizing Spiritual Awareness

To the LORD, who grants Netzach in the form of immortality to the nation of Israel. A psalm of David.

I will always praise you, LORD, and tell the nations of your wondrous works in good and bad times.

I rejoice and sing praises to your name, O most high.

When Goliath was slain, the Philistines stumbled back home because they were in fear of Gevurah. Justice for Israel was being served because of the Philistines oppression.

You have furthered my destiny and appointed Gevruah to bring the judgment seat for judging righteously.

For you have told the nations of the world that lawlessness and immorality will eventually bring Gevurah to the nation, and the nation will be erased from history.

The enemy's kingdom has come to an end forever. You destroyed their cities, and they have been removed from history and thus forgotten.

The LORD is resting until the defeat of Amalek, for when that happens, Gevurah will judge the world from His throne.

And Gevurah will judge the world and will bring order to chaos through executing judgment upon the nations.

The LORD shall become a high tower for the oppressed and afflicted and for those times of future distress.

The oppressed people who know the LORD's name shall always trust You; You have never forsaken all people who seek out your counsel and help for you.

Sing praises to the LORD who dwells in the Temple in Zion, and declare His works among the nations.

For the LORD, avenges blood has remembered them; He has not forgotten the cry of the humble.

Favor me, LORD. See my afflictions and give me a generous portion of mercy for you alone raise me above death's door.

That I may tell of Your acts and that I may take one-day rejoice within the gates of Zion, so that I may rejoice in your salvation.

Whenever a nation falls into their own evil pit, into the very snare they caught their foot in,

The LORD becomes known because He sends Gevurah to execute judgment. Meditate on these two verses.

All the nations that have not lived according to the LORD's moral laws will retreat through Gehinnom toward Sheol.

For the pauper shall not eternally be forgotten, nor shall the hope of the oppressed perish.

Arise LORD and do not let the oppressors prevail as you send Gevurah to intervene in their doing.

PSALM TEN

Language

New American Standard 1995	Hebrew
[1] Why do You stand afar off, O LORD? Why do You hide *Yourself* in times of trouble? [2] In pride the wicked hotly pursue the afflicted; Let them be caught in the plots which they have devised. [3] For the wicked boasts of his heart's desire, And the greedy man curses *and* spurns the LORD. [4] The wicked, in the haughtiness of his countenance, does not seek *Him*. All his thoughts are, "There is no God." [5] His ways prosper at all times; Your judgments are on high, out of his sight; As for all his adversaries, he snorts at them. [6] He says to himself, "I will not be moved; Throughout all generations I will not be in adversity." [7] His mouth is full of curses and deceit and oppression; Under his tongue is mischief and wickedness. [8] He sits in the lurking places of the villages; In the hiding places he kills the innocent; His eyes stealthily watch for the unfortunate. [9] He lurks in a hiding place as a lion in his lair; He lurks to catch the afflicted; He catches the afflicted when he draws him into his net. [10] He crouches, he bows down, And the unfortunate fall by his mighty ones.	לָמָה יְהוָה תַּעֲמֹד בְּרָחוֹק תַּעְלִים לְעִתּוֹת בַּצָּרָה׃ 2 בְּגַאֲוַת רָשָׁע יִדְלַק עָנִי יִתָּפְשׂוּ בִּמְזִמּוֹת זוּ חָשָׁבוּ׃ 3 כִּי־הִלֵּל רָשָׁע עַל־תַּאֲוַת נַפְשׁוֹ וּבֹצֵעַ בֵּרֵךְ נִאֵץ יְהוָה׃ 4 רָשָׁע כְּגֹבַהּ אַפּוֹ בַּל־יִדְרֹשׁ אֵין אֱלֹהִים כָּל־מְזִמּוֹתָיו׃ 5 יָחִילוּ דְרָכָו [דְרָכָיו] בְּכָל־עֵת מָרוֹם מִשְׁפָּטֶיךָ מִנֶּגְדּוֹ כָּל־צוֹרְרָיו יָפִיחַ בָּהֶם׃ 6 אָמַר בְּלִבּוֹ בַּל־אֶמּוֹט לְדֹר וָדֹר אֲשֶׁר לֹא־בְרָע׃ 7 אָלָה פִּיהוּ מָלֵא וּמִרְמוֹת וָתֹךְ תַּחַת לְשׁוֹנוֹ עָמָל וָאָוֶן׃ 8 יֵשֵׁב בְּמַאְרַב חֲצֵרִים בַּמִּסְתָּרִים יַהֲרֹג נָקִי עֵינָיו לְחֵלְכָה יִצְפֹּנוּ׃ 9 יֶאֱרֹב בַּמִּסְתָּר כְּאַרְיֵה בְסֻכֹּה יֶאֱרֹב לַחֲטוֹף עָנִי יַחְטֹף עָנִי בְּמָשְׁכוֹ בְרִשְׁתּוֹ׃ 10 וְדָכָה [יִדְכֶּה] יָשֹׁחַ וְנָפַל בַּעֲצוּמָיו חֵלְכָּאִים [חֵיל]׃ 11 אָמַר [כָּאִים]׃ בְּלִבּוֹ שָׁכַח אֵל הִסְתִּיר פָּנָיו בַּל־רָאָה לָנֶצַח׃ 12 קוּמָה יְהוָה אֵל נְשָׂא יָדֶךָ אַל־תִּשְׁכַּח עֲנָוִים [עֲנִיִּים]׃ 13 עַל־מֶה נִאֵץ רָשָׁע

¹¹ He says to himself, "God has forgotten; He has hidden His face; He will never see it."

¹² Arise, O LORD; O God, lift up Your hand. Do not forget the afflicted.

¹³ Why has the wicked spurned God? He has said to himself, "You will not require *it*."

¹⁴ You have seen *it*, for You have beheld mischief and vexation to take it into Your hand. The unfortunate commits *himself* to You; You have been the helper of the orphan.

¹⁵ Break the arm of the wicked and the evildoer, Seek out his wickedness until You find none.

¹⁶ The LORD is King forever and ever; Nations have perished from His land.

¹⁷ O LORD, You have heard the desire of the humble; You will strengthen their heart, You will incline Your ear

¹⁸ To vindicate the orphan and the oppressed, So that man who is of the earth will no longer cause terror.

אֱלֹהִים אָמַר בְּלִבּוֹ לֹא תִדְרֹשׁ ׃ 14

רָאִתָה כִּי־אַתָּה עָמָל וָכַעַס ׀

תַּבִּיט לָתֵת בְּיָדֶךָ עָלֶיךָ יַעֲזֹב

חֵלֶכָה יָתוֹם אַתָּה הָיִיתָ עוֹזֵר ׃ 15

שְׁבֹר זְרוֹעַ רָשָׁע וָרָע תִּדְרוֹשׁ־

רִשְׁעוֹ בַל־תִּמְצָא ׃ 16 יְהוָה מֶלֶךְ

עוֹלָם וָעֶד אָבְדוּ גוֹיִם מֵאַרְצוֹ ׃ 17

תַּאֲוַת עֲנָוִים שָׁמַעְתָּ יְהוָה תָּכִין

לִבָּם תַּקְשִׁיב אָזְנֶךָ ׃ 18 לִשְׁפֹּט יָתוֹם

וָדָךְ בַּל־יוֹסִיף עוֹד לַעֲרֹץ אֱנוֹשׁ

מִן־הָאָרֶץ ׃

Psa. 10:1 Why, O LORD, will you stand afar off, hide yourself in the dwelling of the holy ones in the times of distress? **2** In brutality the wicked man will pursue the poor man; they will be caught in the scheme that they plotted to carry out. **3** For the wicked man is praised for the craving of his soul; he who blesses the violent man abhors the word of the LORD. **4** The wicked man in the grossness of his spirit will not seek God, and he will say in his heart that his thoughts are not manifest in the presence of the LORD. **5** His ways prosper at all times; your judgments are far from his sight; he will rebuke all his oppressors. **6** He will say in his heart, "I will not be shaken from doing evil for all generations." **7** His mouth is curses, full of guile and deceit; under his tongue is misery and falsehood. **8** He will sit in the hiding places of the courtyards; in secret places he will kill the innocent; he will hide his eyes against the poor. **9** He will lie in wait in secret places like a lion in his covert; he will lie in wait to seize the poor man; he will seize the poor man when he is drawn into his trap. **10** The poor man will be crushed, and sink down, and he will fall into the power of his hiding places. **11** He will say in his heart, "God has forgotten, he has hidden his face, he does not see forever." **12** Arise, O LORD, fulfill the oath of your hand, do not forget the humble. **13** Why has the wicked man abhorred God? He will say in his heart, "It will not be sought after." **14** It is manifest in your presence, because you will inflict misery and wrath upon the wicked man; look carefully to pay a good reward to the righteous by your hand; the poor will place their hope on you; you have been a helper to the orphan. **15** Break the arm of the wicked; and let the evil seek their wickedness, [and] not find it. **16** The LORD is king forever and ever; the Gentiles have perished from his land. **17** The desire of the humble is heard in your presence, O LORD; strengthen their heart, incline your ear. **18** To judge the orphan and poor man; may the sons of men not again be shattered before the wicked of the earth. --

<h1 style="text-align:center">Verse One</h1>

New American Standard 1995	Hebrew
[1] Why do You stand afar off, O LORD? Why do You hide *Yourself* in times of trouble?	לָמָה יְהוָה תַּעֲמֹד בְּרָחוֹק תַּעְלִים לְעִתּוֹת בַּצָּרָה׃

Verse Analysis

Psalm 10 discusses human relationships. In particular, it addresses the thinking of an individual who has thrown off the yoke of moral and ethical laws. It is hoped that the LORD will break the unchecked power to a point where they cannot hurt anyone else. The people felt that the LORD was far away when the ordinary people suffered.

Verse Rewrite Emphasizing Spiritual Awareness

Why, in times of trouble, does it seem that you are not with me?

Verse Two

New American Standard 1995	Hebrew
[2] In pride the wicked hotly pursue the afflicted; Let them be caught in the plots which they have devised.	בְּגַאֲוַת רָשָׁע יִדְלַק עָנִי יִתָּפְשׂוּ ׀ 2 ׃ בִּמְזִמּוֹת זוּ חָשָׁבוּ ׃

Verse Analysis

In general, a person who is dependent upon another for his existence becomes submissive to that person's will. It is pride and arrogance which causes a person not to bow down to a "higher" power. When a person disobeys the LORD, he is arrogant because the LORD is far more powerful. The human ego tends to do this. Pride opens the soul to Evil inclination.

Verse Rewrite Emphasizing Spiritual Awareness

May the LORD place the oppression of the oppressor on the oppressor.

Verse Three

New American Standard 1995	Hebrew
3 For the wicked boasts of his heart's desire, And the greedy man curses *and* spurns the LORD.	כִּי־הִלֵּל רָשָׁע עַל־תַּאֲוַת נַפְשׁוֹ וּבֹצֵעַ בֵּרֵךְ נִאֵץ ׀ יְהוָה

Verse Analysis

The wicked and greedy see their material possession as something that he has won on their own. The people who believe in the LORD know that what they have materially is a blessing granted to them by the LORD.

Verse Rewrite Emphasizing Spiritual Awareness

The wicked and greedy boast that all he possesses were because of his abilities.

Verse Four

New American Standard 1995	Hebrew
[4] The wicked, in the haughtiness of his countenance, does not seek *Him*. All his thoughts are, "There is no God."	רָשָׁע כְּגֹבַהּ אַפּוֹ בַּל־יִדְרֹשׁ אֵין אֱלֹהִים כָּל־מְזִמּוֹתָיו׃

Verse Analysis

אַפּוֹ (afo) – means "nose." It can also mean "anger." If one holds his countenance high above all others, he holds their nose above other people. Such people do not believe that the LORD exists.

Verse Rewrite Emphasizing Spiritual Awareness

People who do not believe in the LORD do not seek Him.

Verse Five

New American Standard 1995	Hebrew
⁵ His ways prosper at all times; Your judgments are on high, out of his sight; As for all his adversaries, he snorts at them.	5 יָחִ֣ילוּ דְרָכָ֨ו ׀ [דְרָכָ֬יו] בְּכָל־עֵ֗ת מָר֤וֹם מִ֭שְׁפָּטֶיךָ מִנֶּגְדּ֑וֹ כָּל־צ֝וֹרְרָ֗יו יָפִ֥יחַ בָּהֶֽם׃

Verse Analysis

This verse describes a person who does not fear justice from the LORD. Why? Because everything that he does is prosperous materialistically. This type of person does not understand that there is a spiritual world. When his time in Malkhut is over, he does not understand that the soul will enter the spiritual world of Yesod.

An evil person who cheats and steals gains materialistic property but sacrifices their soul.

Verse Rewrite Emphasizing Spiritual Awareness

An evil person prospers all the time. The LORD's judgment is unknown to him.

Verse Six

New American Standard 1995	Hebrew
[6] He says to himself, "I will not be moved; Throughout all generations I will not be in adversity."	אָמַר בְּלִבּוֹ בַּל־אֶמּוֹט לְדֹר וָדֹר אֲשֶׁר לֹא־בְרָע

Verse Analysis

Even in bad times or misfortunes, the wicked still thrive.

Verse Rewrite Emphasizing Spiritual Awareness

He says to himself, "No matter what bad times or misfortunes come, the wicked still thrive."

Verse Seven

New American Standard 1995	Hebrew
7 His mouth is full of curses and deceit and oppression; Under his tongue is mischief and wickedness.	אָלָה פִּיהוּ מָלֵא וּמִרְמוֹת וָתֹךְ 7 תַּחַת לְשׁוֹנוֹ עָמָל וָאָוֶן׃

Verse Analysis

אָלָה (ala) – means "to swear." This word is used when a person swears or curses against the LORD. This verse says that this person may say righteous things, which is on the tip of his tongue, but the truth is that he remains evil. When a wicked person wants to deceive, he will create an oath that he has no intention to fulfill.

Verse Rewrite Emphasizing Spiritual Awareness

His mouth is full of oaths and behind these false oaths is his wickedness.

Verse Eight

New American Standard 1995	Hebrew
[8] He sits in the lurking places of the villages; In the hiding places he kills the innocent; His eyes stealthily watch for the unfortunate.	‏יֵשֵׁב ׀ בְּמַאְרַב חֲצֵרִים 8 ׃ בַּמִּסְתָּרִים יַהֲרֹג נָקִי עֵינָיו לְחֵלְכָה יִצְפֹּנוּ

Verse Analysis

"He sits in the lurking places of the villages" means to make oneself at home in domestic circles and to become well-acquainted with the most intimate affairs of families utilizing social intercourse with the inhabitants of the neighborhood.

Verse Rewrite Emphasizing Spiritual Awareness

He becomes accepted by the families of a village but then kills the innocent and is watching to take advantage of the weak.

Verse Nine

New American Standard 1995	Hebrew
[9] He lurks in a hiding place as a lion in his lair; He lurks to catch the afflicted; He catches the afflicted when he draws him into his net.	יֶאֱרֹב בַּמִּסְתָּר ׀ כְּאַרְיֵה בְסֻכֹּה 9 יֶאֱרֹב לַחֲטוֹף עָנִי יַחְטֹף עָנִי בְּמָשְׁכוֹ בְרִשְׁתּוֹ

Verse Analysis

בְסֻכֹּה - (b'sookoo) means "in his lair." This word is actually written in the feminine form. However, the Masoretic point system is being violated in this verse. The wrong point has been placed on the "cuf." This indicates that the author wanted to express that this male person was hiding his real strength by acting like a woman. Since women are weaker than men, this interpretation is valid. The person who is hiding is preparing to attack the poor and abuse them.

Verse Rewrite Emphasizing Spiritual Awareness

He lies in wait, looking like a weak and peaceful lion; when he can, he will ensnare a poor person to abuse and rob him.

Verse Ten

New American Standard 1995	Hebrew
[10] He crouches, he bows down, And the unfortunate fall by his mighty ones.	10 וְדָכָה [וְדִכֶּה] יָשֹׁחַ וְנָפַל בַּעֲצוּמָיו חֵלְכָּאִים [חֵיל] [כָּאִים׃]

Verse Analysis

The person who preys on the poor is considered wicked and a low person morally. A lowly person bows down to a mightier person.

Verse Rewrite Emphasizing Spiritual Awareness

He acts as a humble man; he walks bowed down until the hosts of the weak fall victim to his ways of violence.

Verse Eleven

New American Standard 1995	Hebrew
[11] He says to himself, "God has forgotten; He has hidden His face; He will never see it."	אָמַר בְּלִבּוֹ שָׁכַח אֵל הִסְתִּיר פָּנָיו בַּל־רָאָה לָנֶצַח׃

Verse Analysis

This verse says that the refusal to believe in the LORD's providence in historical events is what the wicked believe. They also believe that the LORD does not see what they are doing. Thus, at the Tikkun, they will not be judged for their evil while on the Earth. They would not believe in a final judgment.

Verse Rewrite Emphasizing Spiritual Awareness

He says to himself, "The LORD will never see our evil because I do not believe in His existence."

Verse Twelve

New American Standard 1995	Hebrew
[12] Arise, O LORD; O God, lift up Your hand. Do not forget the afflicted.	קוּמָה יְהוָה אֵל נְשָׂא יָדֶךָ אַל־ תִּשְׁכַּח עֲנִיִּים [עֲנָוִים:]

Verse Analysis

The Psalmist is asking the LORD to defend the afflicted and the poor.

Verse Rewrite Emphasizing Spiritual Awareness

Arise LORD and by your Hand help the afflicted.

<h1 style="text-align:center">Verse Thirteen and Fourteen</h1>

New American Standard 1995	Hebrew
[13] Why has the wicked spurned God? He has said to himself, "You will not require *it*." [14] You have seen *it,* for You have beheld mischief and vexation to take it into Your hand. The unfortunate commits *himself* to You; You have been the helper of the orphan.	עַל־מֶה ׀ נִאֵץ רָשָׁע ׀ אֱלֹהִים אָמַר רָאֹתָה כִּי־אַתָּה עָמָל וָכַעַס ׀ תַּבִּיט לָתֵת בְּיָדֶךָ עָלֶיךָ יַעֲזֹב

Verse Analysis

The lawless man mocks the LORD by disobeying His Law and thinks that the LORD is not concerned about humankind.

Verse Rewrite Emphasizing Spiritual Awareness

V.13 – Why does the wicked person mock the LORD? He says in his heart, "The LORD does not care about us."

V. 14 – But You have seen this lawlessness; all things are in Your hands; You have been the helper of the orphan.

<h1 style="text-align:center">Verse Fifteen</h1>

New American Standard 1995	Hebrew
¹⁵ Break the arm of the wicked and the evildoer, Seek out his wickedness until You find none.	שְׁבֹר זְרוֹעַ רָשָׁע וָרָע תִּדְרוֹשׁ־רִשְׁעוֹ בַל־תִּמְצָא׃

Verse Analysis

The Psalmist asked the LORD to seek out evil and punish it. When this is complete evil will be banished from the Earth.

Verse Rewrite Emphasizing Spiritual Awareness

LORD, remove the wicked from the Earth so that You will not find it here anymore.

Verse Sixteen

New American Standard 1995	Hebrew
[16] The LORD is King forever and ever; Nations have perished from His land.	יְהוָה מֶלֶךְ עוֹלָם וָעֶד אָבְדוּ גוֹיִם מֵאַרְצוֹ

Verse Analysis

One day the LORD's sovereignty will be acknowledged everywhere.

Verse Rewrite Emphasizing Spiritual Awareness

The LORD is King forever; however, the nations of the Earth will one day perish.

Verse Seventeen

New American Standard 1995	Hebrew
[17] O LORD, You have heard the desire of the humble; You will strengthen their heart, You will incline Your ear	תַּאֲוַת עֲנָוִים שָׁמַעְתָּ יְהוָה תָּכִין לִבָּם תַּקְשִׁיב אָזְנֶךָ :

Verse Analysis

The LORD has always heard the voice of the humble and poor. LORD, you can strengthen the humble.

Verse Rewrite Emphasizing Spiritual Awareness

LORD, You have heard the desire of the humble; now guide their hearts and hear their cries for help.

Verse Eighteen

New American Standard 1995	Hebrew
[18] To vindicate the orphan and the oppressed, So that man who is of the earth will no longer cause terror.	לִשְׁפֹּט יָתוֹם וָדָךְ בַּל־יוֹסִיף עוֹד לַעֲרֹץ אֱנוֹשׁ מִן־הָאָרֶץ׃

Verse Analysis

The LORD always champions the orphan and poor.

Verse Rewrite Emphasizing Spiritual Awareness

Champion the orphans and the oppressed so that the men of violence will not continue to spread their terror around the Earth.

Complete Psalm Rewrite Emphasizing Spiritual Awareness

Why, in times of trouble, does it seem that you are not with me?

May the LORD place the oppression of the oppressor on the oppressor.

The wicked and greedy boast that all he possesses were because of his abilities.

People who do not believe in the LORD do not seek Him.

An evil person prospers all the time. The LORD's judgment is unknown to him.

He says to himself, "No matter what bad times or misfortunes come, the wicked still thrive."

His mouth is full of oaths and behind these false oaths is his wickedness.

He becomes accepted by the families of a village but then kills the innocent and is watching to take advantage of the weak.

He lies in wait, looking like a weak and peaceful lion; when he can, he will ensnare a poor person to abuse and rob him.

He acts as a humble man; he walks bowed down until the hosts of the weak fall victim to his ways of violence.

He says to himself, "The LORD will never see our evil because I do not believe in His existence."

Arise LORD and by your Hand help the afflicted.

Why does the wicked person mock the LORD? He says in his heart, "The LORD does not care about us."

But You have seen this lawlessness; all things are in Your hands; You have been the helper of the orphan.

LORD, remove the wicked from the Earth so that You will not find it here anymore.

The LORD is King forever; however, the nations of the Earth will one day perish.

LORD, You have heard the desire of the humble; now guide their hearts and hear their cries for help.

Champion the orphans and the oppressed so that the men of violence will not continue to spread their terror around the Earth.

APPENDIX

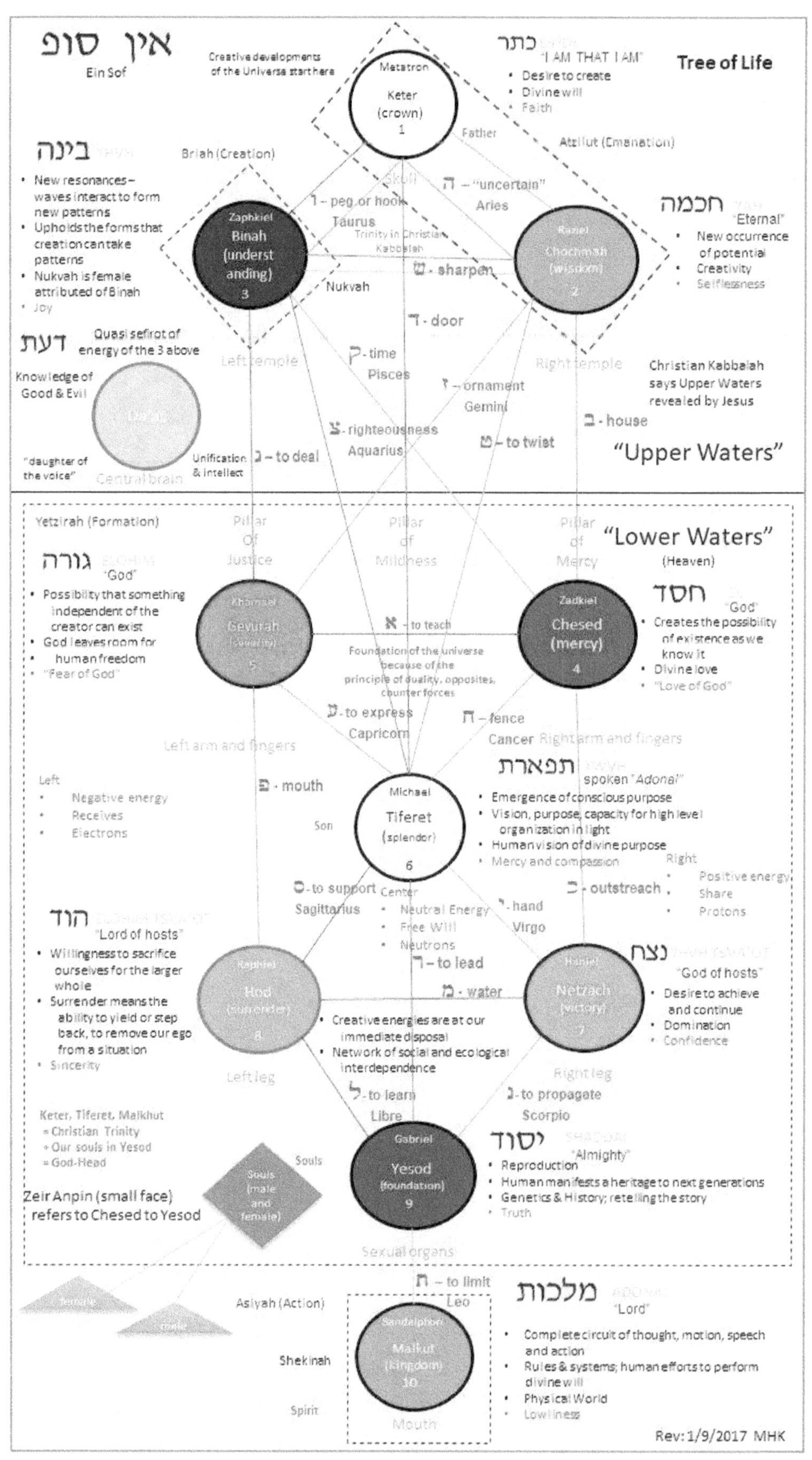

אין סוף
Ein Sof
Tree of Life
Creative developments of the Universe start here
"I AM THAT I AM"
• Desire to create
• Divine will
• Faith
Metatron
Keter (crown)
1
Father
Atzilut (Emanation)
Briah (Creation)
בינה
• New resonances – waves interact to form new patterns
• Upholds the forms that creation can take patterns
• Nukvah is female attributed of Binah
• Joy
Zaphkiel
Binah (understanding)
3
ו – peg or hook
Taurus
Trinity in Christian Kabbalah
ש - sharpen
Nukvah
ה – "uncertain"
Aries
חכמה
"Eternal"
• New occurrence of potential
• Creativity
• Selflessness
Raziel
Chochmah (wisdom)
2
דעת
Quasi sefirot of energy of the 3 above
Knowledge of Good & Evil
"daughter of the voice"
Da'at
Central brain
Unification & intellect
ד - door
ק - time
Pisces
ז – ornament
Gemini
צ - righteousness
Aquarius
נ – to deal
ב - house
ט – to twist
Christian Kabbalah says Upper Waters revealed by Jesus
"Upper Waters"
Left temple
Right temple
Yetzirah (Formation)
Pillar Of Justice
Pillar of Mildness
Pillar of Mercy
"Lower Waters"
(Heaven)
גורה
"God"
• Possibility that something independent of the creator can exist
• God leaves room for human freedom
• "Fear of God"
Khamael
Gevurah (severity)
5
א - to teach
Foundation of the universe because of the principle of duality, opposites, counter forces
חסד
"God"
• Creates the possibility of existence as we know it
• Divine love
• "Love of God"
Zadkiel
Chesed (mercy)
4
ע - to express
Capricorn
ח – fence
Cancer
Right arm and fingers
Left arm and fingers
Left
• Negative energy
• Receives
• Electrons
תפארת
spoken "Adonai"
• Emergence of conscious purpose
• Vision, purpose, capacity for high level organization in light
• Human vision of divine purpose
• Mercy and compassion
Michael
Tiferet (splendor)
6
Son
פ - mouth
ס - to support
Sagittarius
Center
• Neutral Energy
• Free Will
• Neutrons
י – hand
Virgo
Right
• Positive energy
• Share
• Protons
כ - outstreach
הוד
"Lord of hosts"
• Willingness to sacrifice ourselves for the larger whole
• Surrender means the ability to yield or step back, to remove our ego from a situation
• Sincerity
Raphiel
Hod (surrender)
8
Left leg
ר – to lead
מ - water
Creative energies are at our immediate disposal
Network of social and ecological interdependence
נצח
"God of hosts"
• Desire to achieve and continue
• Domination
• Confidence
Haniel
Netzach (victory)
7
Right leg
ל – to learn
Libre
ג - to propagate
Scorpio
Keter, Tiferet, Malkhut
= Christian Trinity
+ Our souls in Yesod
= God-Head
Zeir Anpin (small face) refers to Chesed to Yesod
Souls
Souls (male and female)
Gabriel
Yesod (foundation)
9
יסוד
"Almighty"
• Reproduction
• Human manifests a heritage to next generations
• Genetics & History; retelling the story
• Truth
Sexual organs
female
male
Aslyah (Action)
Shekinah
Spirit
ת – to limit
Leo
Sandalphon
Malkut (kingdom)
10
מלכות
"Lord"
• Complete circuit of thought, motion, speech and action
• Rules & systems; human efforts to perform divine will
• Physical World
• Lowliness
Mouth
Rev: 1/9/2017 MHK

Mystical Methodology to Prayer

All prayers result in spiritual energy which rises through the conduits that connect Sefirot realms. The "answer" to prayers is the transformation of spiritual energy from its original frequency to an appropriate frequency which will give the necessary results.

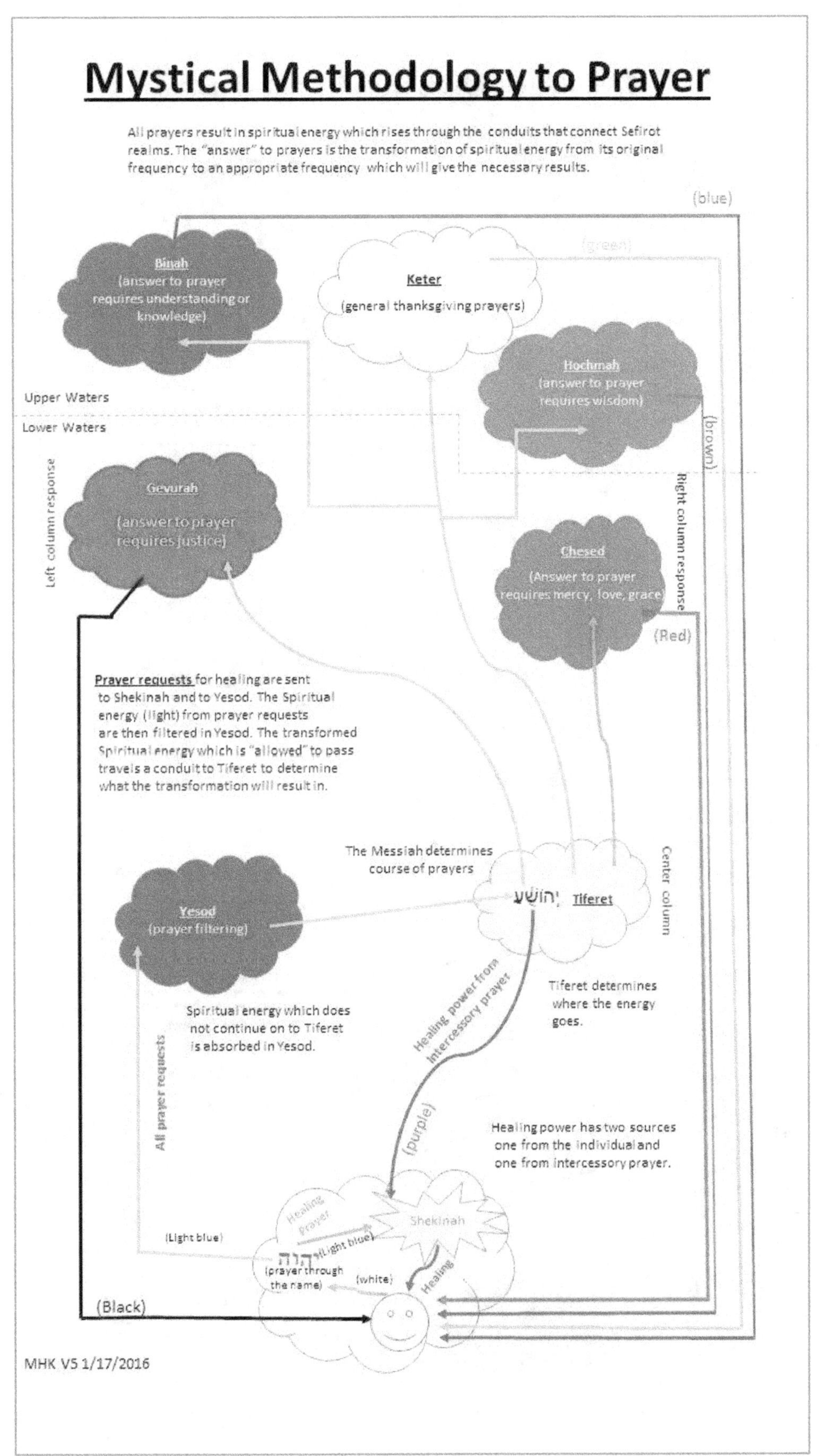

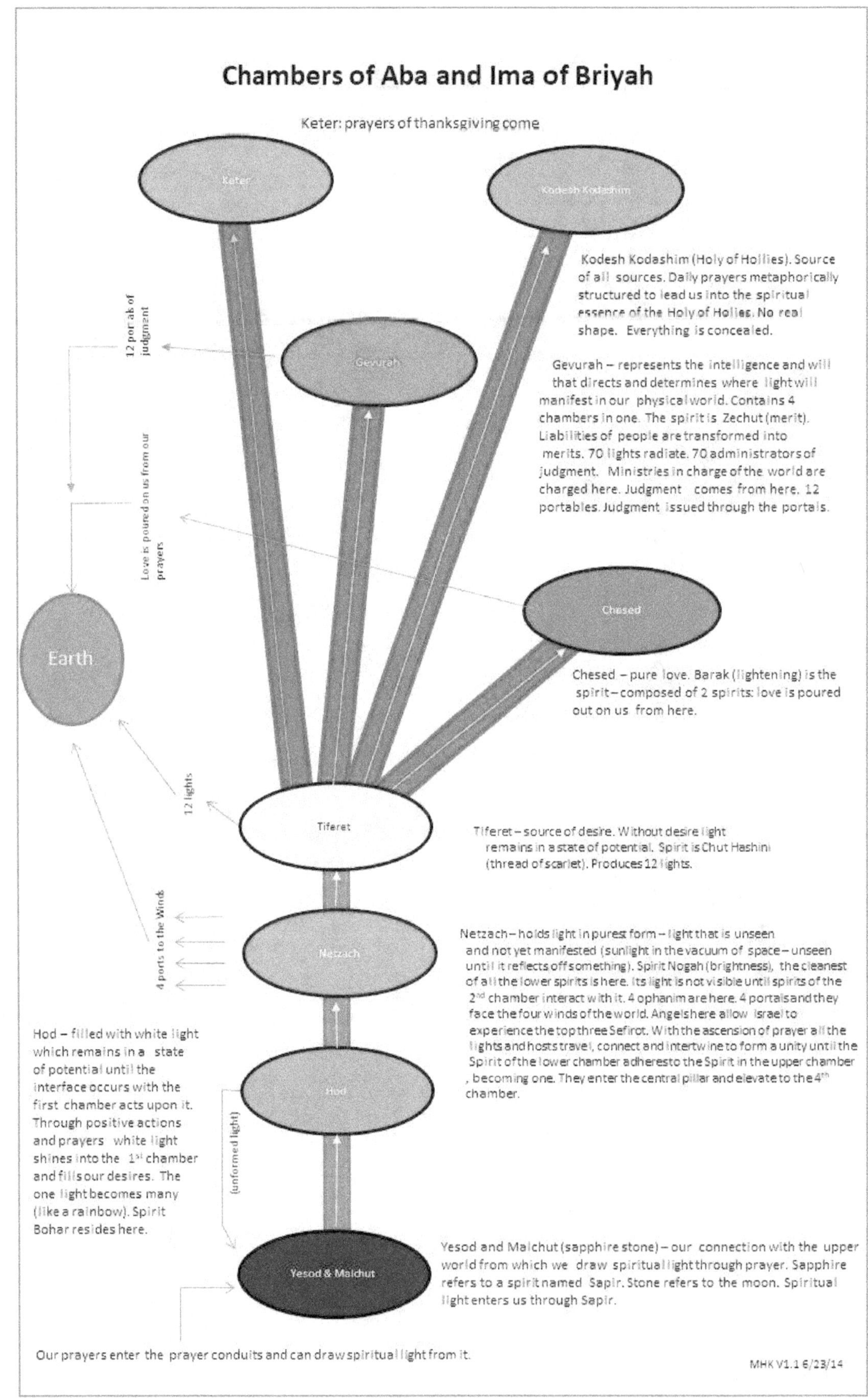

Chambers of Aba and Ima of Briyah

Keter: prayers of thanksgiving come

Keter

Kodesh Kodashim

Gevurah

Chesed

Earth

Tiferet

Netzach

Hod

Yesod & Malchut

12 portals of judgment

Love is poured on us from our prayers

12 lights

4 ports to the Winds

(unformed light)

Kodesh Kodashim (Holy of Hollies). Source of all sources. Daily prayers metaphorically structured to lead us into the spiritual essence of the Holy of Holies. No real shape. Everything is concealed.

Gevurah – represents the intelligence and will that directs and determines where light will manifest in our physical world. Contains 4 chambers in one. The spirit is Zechut (merit). Liabilities of people are transformed into merits. 70 lights radiate. 70 administrators of judgment. Ministries in charge of the world are charged here. Judgment comes from here. 12 portables. Judgment issued through the portals.

Chesed – pure love. Barak (lightening) is the spirit – composed of 2 spirits: love is poured out on us from here.

Tiferet – source of desire. Without desire light remains in a state of potential. Spirit is Chut Hashini (thread of scarlet). Produces 12 lights.

Netzach – holds light in purest form – light that is unseen and not yet manifested (sunlight in the vacuum of space – unseen until it reflects off something). Spirit Nogah (brightness), the cleanest of all the lower spirits is here. Its light is not visible until spirits of the 2nd chamber interact with it. 4 ophanim are here. 4 portals and they face the four winds of the world. Angels here allow Israel to experience the top three Sefirot. With the ascension of prayer all the lights and hosts travel, connect and intertwine to form a unity until the Spirit of the lower chamber adheres to the Spirit in the upper chamber, becoming one. They enter the central pillar and elevate to the 4th chamber.

Hod – filled with white light which remains in a state of potential until the interface occurs with the first chamber acts upon it. Through positive actions and prayers white light shines into the 1st chamber and fills our desires. The one light becomes many (like a rainbow). Spirit Bohar resides here.

Yesod and Malchut (sapphire stone) – our connection with the upper world from which we draw spiritual light through prayer. Sapphire refers to a spirit named Sapir. Stone refers to the moon. Spiritual light enters us through Sapir.

Our prayers enter the prayer conduits and can draw spiritual light from it.

MHK V1.1 6/23/14

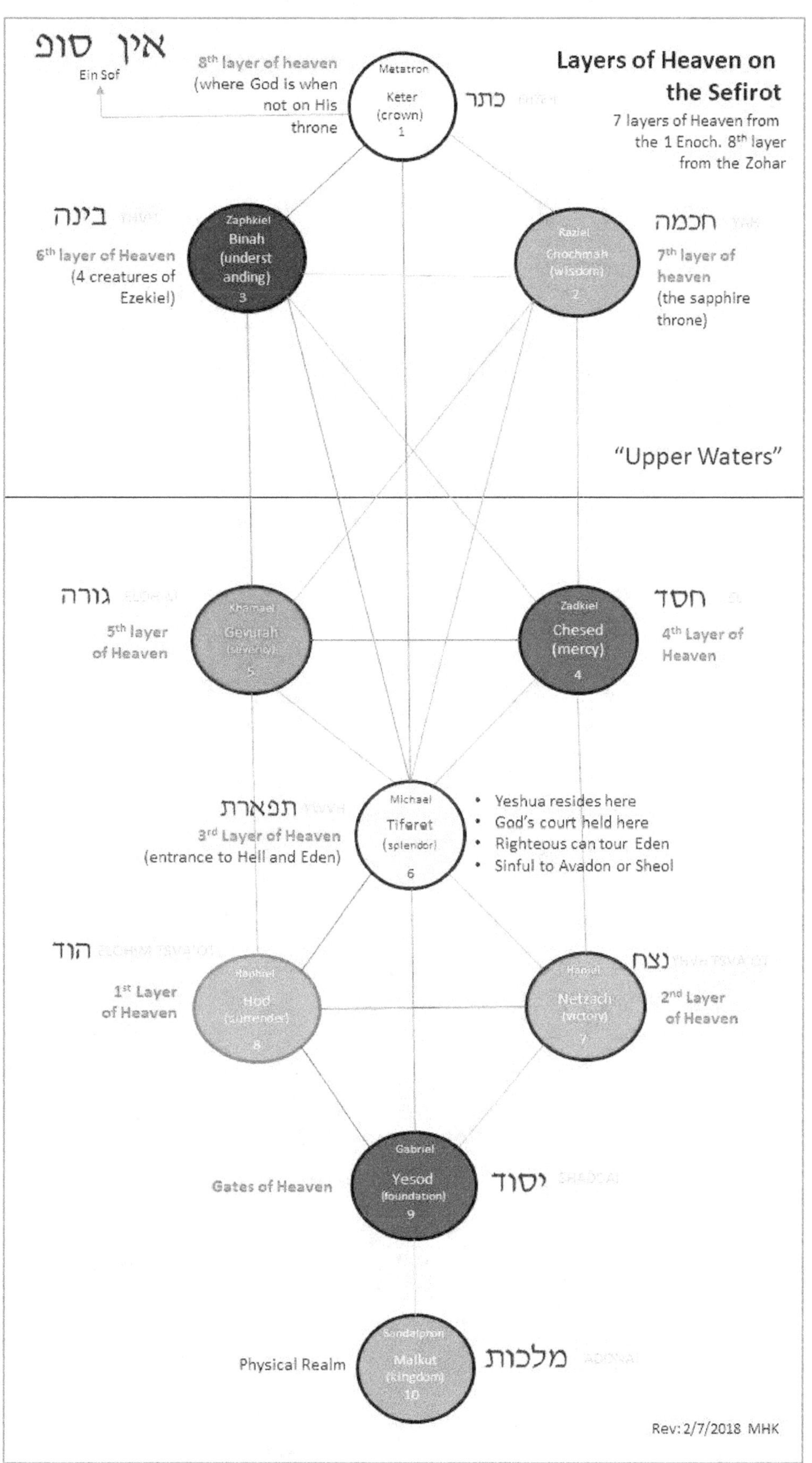

אין סוף
Ein Sof
8th layer of heaven (where God is when not on His throne)
Metatron
Keter (crown)
1
כתר
Layers of Heaven on the Sefirot
7 layers of Heaven from the 1 Enoch. 8th layer from the Zohar
בינה
6th layer of Heaven (4 creatures of Ezekiel)
Zaphkiel
Binah (understanding)
3
חכמה
Raziel
Chochmah (wisdom)
2
7th layer of heaven (the sapphire throne)
"Upper Waters"
גורה
5th layer of Heaven
Khamael
Gevurah (severity)
5
חסד
Zadkiel
Chesed (mercy)
4
4th Layer of Heaven
תפארת
3rd Layer of Heaven (entrance to Hell and Eden)
Michael
Tiferet (splendor)
6
• Yeshua resides here
• God's court held here
• Righteous can tour Eden
• Sinful to Avadon or Sheol
הוד
1st Layer of Heaven
Raphael
Hod (surrender)
8
נצח
Haniel
Netzach (victory)
7
2nd Layer of Heaven
Gabriel
Yesod (foundation)
9
Gates of Heaven
יסוד
Sandalphon
Malkut (kingdom)
10
Physical Realm
מלכות
Rev: 2/7/2018 MHK